🛡 Berkeley College™

From the Library

of

WESTCHESTER CAMPUS

99 CHURCH STREET
WHITE PLAINS, NY 10601

S0-BSF-179

THE TWENTIETH CENTURY
FASHION SERIES

edited by
Ieri Attualità

THE TWENTIETH CENTURY
FASHION SERIES

WOMAN

1. Evening dresses 1900...1940 (Marco Tosa) *
2. Evening dresses 1940...   (Marco Tosa) *
3. Maternity clothes (Doretta Davanzo Poli) *
4. Skirts & more skirts (Fiora Gandolfi) *
5. Costume jewellery
6. Parthy Shoes (Luciana Boccardi) *
7. Suits and daywear
8. Strictly personal: corsets and brassières
9. Nightwear
10. Trousers for women
11. Day and evening bags
12. Blouses
13. Large and small hats
14. Tricot and jersey fashion
15. Hosiery and related items
16. Gloves
17. Cloaks and coats
18. Fard and powder
19. Hairstyles
20. Casual shoes and boots
21. Ladies in furs 1900 -1940 (Anna Municchi) *
22. Ladies in furs 1940 -1990 (Anna Municchi) *
23. Afternoon and cocktail dress
24. Beachwear and swimsuits (Doretta Davanzo Poli) *
25. Shawls, scarfs and silk squares
26. Bridal gowns (V. de Buzzaccarini - D. Davanzo Poli) *
27. Details: necks and necklines
28. Details: sleeves
29. A Century of fashion on movies

CHILDREN

30. Babies
31. Girls
32. Children and brats
33. Dressed up for a party (Nora Villa) *
34. Teenage boys
35. Teenage girls

MEN

36. Underwear
37. Shirts
38. Men's accessories: belts, gloves, ties and scarf
39. Waistcoats
40. Men's hats (G. Folledore) *
41. Furs for men (Anna Municchi) *
42. Trousers & Co. (V. de Buzzaccarini) *
43. Men's jewellery
44. Overcoats and coats
45. Pyjamas, robes etc.
46. Knitwear: cardigan and pullovers
47. Men's Coats (V. de Buzzaccarini) *
48. Hairstyles, beards and mustaches
49. Shoes and boots
50. Uniforms
51. Suitcases, briefcases and bags

FABRICS

52. Fabrics in fashion: cotton
53. Fabrics in fashion: wool
54. Fabrics in fashion: silk
55. Fabrics in fashion: man-made fabrics

SPECIAL ITEMS

56. Sportswear
57. Umbrellas, sticks and canes
58. Work clothes
59. Fashion in the rain
60. Embroidery in Fashion
61. Scent and Fashion
62. The andkerchief (Paolo Peri) *
63. Buttons & Soundries (V. de Buzzaccarini - I. Zotti Minici) *
64. Ribbons round the world
65. Leather clothing
66. Jeans
67. T- and polo shirts
68. Glasses (Giuseppe Pellissetti) *

* TENTATIVE TITLES

DORETTA DAVANZO POLI

Beachwear and bathing-costume

Zanfi Editori

ACKNOWLEDGEMENTS

Doretta Davanzo Poli wishes to thank for their kidness and assistence:

Giandomenico Romanelli, Director dei Civici Musei Veneziani
Stefania Moronato, of Centro Studi di Storia del Tessuto e del Costume di
Palazzo Mocenigo, Venezia
Gregory Piazzalunga, vice-president Parah Group
Silvio Belekda,
Beatris Ferretti per La Perla
Laudomia Pucci per Emilio Pucci
Mariapaola De Benedetti
Vittoria de Buzzaccarini
Michaela De Favari
Fiora Gandolfi
Fondazione Ken Scott
Emenda Marinelli
Chiara Padovano
Cicci Rippa Bonatti
Angelo Secchi
Jacopo Valli

This book was made possible by a
contribution from **Parah Group**

Series editor: Vittoria de Buzzaccarini
Historical and iconographic research: Doretta Davanzo Poli
Editorial: Chiara Padovano
Lay-out: Michaela De Favari
Photographic reproduction: Giuliano Grossi
Production: Costantino Bergamini

The English edition:
Translated by: Frederic Hurdis Jones and Katia Padovani
Edited by: Katia Padovani

All rights reserved. No part of this book may be reproduced, memorized by
computer or trasmitted in any form or manner, mechanical, electronic,
photographic or otherwise without the publisher's express written authorisation.
Any infringements or violations shall be subject to legal action under Italian law
and international copyright conventions.

© 1995 **Zanfi** Editori s.r.l.
via Emilia Ovest 954 - 41100 Modena (Italy)
Tel. 059/891700 - Telefax 059/891701

I ISBN 88-86169-83-3
Il Novecento
Periodico - Aut. Trib. di Modena n. 904 del 18/01/88
Sped. abb. post. GR III/70
Direttore responsabile: Celestino Zanfi

INDEX

... to Massimo, Enrico e Teresa

D.D.P.

*I wish to sincerely thank Doretta Davanzo Poli, who
accepted my request to write a book on the
history of bathing-costumes - which was never
written in Italy - and who produced such
a comprehensive work.
To all bathing-suit fans, fashion experts and readers,
with the hope to have contributed to the hist
ory and culture of beachware, a sector that
deserves to be better known.*

Gregory Piazzalunga
Vice-president Parah Group

FROM DIANA TO MARIE ANTOINETTE

1. The first girls to wear bikinis. 3rd century A.D. mosaic, Piazza Armerina, Sicily.

2.

BEACHWEAR THE ROMANS DID IT

The huge annual summer mass-migration to the beaches found its singer, in the 1980's, in Gabriella Ferri, who incited her television audiences with her refrain of "Let's all run to the beach!".

However, running to the beach is no ancient custom.

Although there is no evidence that they plunged into the sea itself or wore special clothes for doing so (and in any event such a habit disappeared completely with the barbarian invasions) the Romans, of course, went frequently to the public baths and their adjoining gymnasiums, but as these ablutions were undertaken for reasons of cleanliness; or care for one's body, there was no exhibiting of special garments for the purpose.

The first bathing-suit (or at least something very like that worn by 20th century ladies) of which we have a representation in the two-piece one so joyfully worn by two young women in a Roman mosaic of the 3rd century A.D., to be seen at Piazza Armerina in Sicily.

The drawers are short enough, but they cover the upper thigh; a broad strip of material covers the breast. Their hair is down in one case and put up in the other, and they wear bracelets on their arms and ankles. They stand in gymnastic attitudes, holding dumb-bells or a ball, and theirs may have been the normal sportswear for young Roman women. There are no other pictures like this in existence.

The myth of Actaeon, a young Greek hunter who came upon Diana and her nymphs bathing in a stream, and who stopped to admire their naked beauty (for which he was turned into a stag and torn to pieces by his own hounds) confirms the fact that the Greeks used to bathe in the nude.

BATHING-DRESSES

Despite their prudery, even the Middle Ages failed to clothe modestly the naked bodies of bathers, although some of them did wear a small triangular cloth over the loins.

Monasteries had no baths at all, and castles rarely included an occasional tub. At the beginning of the Renaissance, Valentina Visconti, Duchess of Orleans, lived in various French castles, and when she moved from one to another she was accompanied by a bath hewn out of a single block of Candolgia marble. This "rose-coloured marble vessel" is mentioned in her trousseau, as well as "a long shift with a belt identifiable as a bathing-dress".

2. In the bath-houses, or stews - the only form of bathing known to our forbears - birthday-suits were the simple costume worn.
Russian Baths by G. Ferrario, *Il costume di tutti i popoli.*

3. Although monks took their baths and saunas naked, girls wore a shirt with shoulder-straps.
Codice d'Ilena, Prague, National Museum.

4. Long tresses covered Venus like a bathing-costume; she is handed a precious cloak to use as a bath-robe.
S. Botticelli, *The birth of Venus.* Uffizi Gallery, Florence.

8

3.

At the same period, Queen Elizabeth of England was prescribed baths in British hot springs as a cure for very painful rheumatism. Cappi Bentivegna tells us: "The Queen halted at the edge of the miracle - working waters ... and hardly deigned to pose her gloved hands on two stout guardsmen's shoulders ... haughtily, with full majesty, she entered the bath, wearing her ruff, her embroidered farthingale and her starched petticoats ... only the crown was lacking".

There is a curious picture by Michelangelo Cerquozzi, "The Roman Bath", painted in about 1650, showing stark-naked young women bathing, trying to swim and sunbathing on the sides of large swimming-baths.

Such a garment, documented from the late 1400's onwards, was a low cut bodice with shoulder-straps and a skirt, often accompanied by a turban as headdress.

Poggio Bracciolini of Florence has left an unusual description of 15th century public baths: "The two sexes are separated by a barrier, but this is provided with little windows, allowing men and women bathers to drink refreshments together, converse and hold hands. Above the bath run balconies, enabling men to look at the women and joke with them. One can sit there and watch the almost naked women entering and emerging from the water". Such costumes as were worn consisted of a thin linen shift, open at the sides and rendered transparent by wetting, so that, according to the writer, it concealed absolutely nothing.

But the beauties of the 16th century went back to classical nude bathing, idealized by contemporary artists who depitcted them as Venus and Diana, nymphs and undines: Botticelli's Venus rises from her shell with no more protection than her luminously flowing hair, and the Susannah with the Elders of Veronese and Tintoretto even dispense with jewellery.

A French taveller named Locatelli recounts that, in the early 17th century, "women in white, black or coloured taffeta used to sit in the park by the banks of the Dora River in Turin on benches in the water, remaining submerged up to the neck".

4.

THE EASY-GOING EIGHTEENTH CENTURY

Toward 1750, the town of Dover was scandalized by the fact that an English lady had allowed herself to be painted on the beach by Thomas Gainsborough wearing a strange costume: a coarse striped cotton smock, like those of mulatto women in the Colonies, a blue fichu and trousers of thick, rigid cloth, held in at the ankles with a broad ribbon. The lady was the actress Sarah Siddons, who was in the habit, when returning from Paris where bathing was becoming all the rage, of stopping at Dover for a dip in the sea.

She was a good swimmer, we are told, although the water filled out her trousers; and the fichu, borne up by the waves, tended to cover her eyes and impair her vision.

At the court of Marie Antoniette, among the delights of the Trianon and the malicious and sometimes fatuous gossip of the Tuileries, the idea of a new pastime was born; that of group-bathing in the park lakes.

In 1750 again, an English doctor called Russel published a Latin treatise on the benefits to be had from sea-water, in which he quoted the famous French naturalist, Georges Louis Buffon. This sent all the aristocracy off to the coasts of Normandy or the French Riviera. A pratical bathing-dress was evolved, consisting of a tunic and trousers of thick, sailor-uniform cloth, to which the less bold ladies added a wide multicoloured skirt, that swelled up like a balloon in the water.

Thanks to a spy in the service of the Inquisitorial Court of Venice, we have the amusing testimony, dated 30 August 1762, concerning the first scandalous bathing-parties held on the Lido.

After saying that it is usually "well-behaved people who go swimming", but that these are always men, and that the women, when any are present, belong to the category of whores, he recalls a recent event which was still giving rise to gossip.

"Two respectable-looking men", "of good standing", followed "by gondoliers in livery" and accompanied by "a beautiful girl wearing a magnificent negligé" undressed on the beach. The men put on

8.

"white shorts", and the girl " a sort of shift that hung down to the ground". Once in the water they indulged in larks of every kind. (G. Comisso).

Then came the Parisian phenomenon of the Merveilleuses of the Directory period. These unprejudiced ladies shortened the trousers hitherto worn, but their "normal" dress was so succinct and transparent that they were better covered when clad for bathing.

5. After bathing in the spring, Susannah, wearing only a pearl bracelet, combs her hair and titivates. Tintoretto, *Susannah and the Elders.* Louvre Museum, Paris.

6. Completely naked, they bathe, chat and take the sun. M. Cercuozzi, c. 1650. *The roman bath,* Rome.

7. Rembrandt's bathing-beauty walks warily, dressed in a bathing-shift.

6.

11

7.

12

8. Her cicisbeo accompanies the lady who, for a stroll by the sea, is wearing a large beribboned bonnet to go with her white taffeta dress. Ca' Rezzonico Museum, Venice. Photo Giacomelli.

8.

THE PRUDISH CENTURY

9. In the Paris of 1800, the smart First Empire bathing-establishment was the Bains Vigier. P.L. de Giafferri, *L'Histoire du Costume Féminin Français.*

14

10.

TRIUMPHANT ENTRY
INTO THE SEA

Laver states that, at the beginning of the 19th century, women bathed in long flannel gowns laced up to the neck and reaching to the feet; in order to avoid the men's wicked glances, they entered the water at some distance from the shore from a boat covered with a large sunshade. Once in the water, the gown floated on the surface, allowing their movements free play but concealing their limbs at the same time.

A red-letter day in the history of the bathing-costume must have been the immersion, in 1812 at Dieppe in France, of Hortense de Beauharnais, Queen of Holland, who had become interested in the therapeutic virtues of sea-bathing. Louis Bonaparte's queen, accompanied by a large suite, entered the water completely clad in long trousers and an ample overall of chocolate-coloured wool.

Dieppe, again, was the scene of a well-described bath taken in July 1824 by the Duchess of Berry, mother of the French pretender who would have succeeded Charles X but for the political and dynastic ambitions of the House of Orleans. We are told that she wore a brown woolen drees with blue piping, a light overgarment, an enormous headdress and low-heeled laced shoes.

The bathing-inspector (some say it was the Préfet in person) gave her his arm, wearing white gloves and a top hat.

The citizenry was warned by a cannon-shot that she had entered the sea, after which an attendant took her up in his arms and carried her into deeper water.

After this, organized bathing for large numbers of people began at Dieppe, soon to be followed by Deauville, Ostend in Belgium and San Sebastian in Spain.

Cappi Bentivegna states that Madame Cleo Cavalli organized a fashion-show for a restricted clientele in 1829 in a smart Roman hotel. She showed her summer models, including a get-up designed by Hortense Allart for bathing at the Acque di Tivoli. It was a masterpiece of inventive boldness: "of light but smooth and rigid taffeta, which the water can swell out without the garment becoming caught up or sticking to the skin, it consisted of a sort of smock complete with trousers; flounces at wrists, neck and ankles provided the immerged body with a

sufficient wall of material for no seductive lines to be seen". The costume was chosen by Cristina Belgioioso, on her way to bathe at Ischia, with the addition of more flounces at the elbows and a fisherman's red sash for her waist.

In those days, women bathers were taken into the sea in cabins with large wheels, in which they changed before their dip.

Naturally, they never showed themselves on the beach in such unbecoming dress. They lived by the seaside in town-clothes of brightly-coloured light material, with gloves, eye-veils and sunshades to protect their skin, which had to remain white, at all coasts.

11.

12.

10. A long white cashmere robe of the *burnous* type, bordered and embroidered, seemed ideal for the practice of "thalassotheraphy". P. L. de Giafferri, op. cit.

11. A complete suit of clothes for bathing, including a straw *capote* hat. Not only were long sleeves worn, but stockings as well. P. L. de Giafferri, op. cit.

12. An 1830 bathing-costume much resembles that worn on the stage by Brighella, a character of the Italian *Commedia dell'Arte*.
Y. Des Landres, *Le costume image de l'homme.*

STANDARDS OF DRESS

Nothing had changed in this respect since the Venice of the 16th century, when the fashion for bleached hair involved long exposure to the sun; but the body was well protected by wide, light clothing (the "schiavonetto"), and the hair to be bleached was arranged all round the brim of a crownless hat. Then, as later, pale skin was a characteristic of the well-to-do, who thus stood out from the others, tanned brown by work in the fields, on the sea, or simply by living for the most part out of doors.

It was not until the second half of the 19th century that doctors began to pay greater attention to the beneficial effects of sunlight, and advised frequent but limited exposure, not only to strengthen the skin, but also to cure certain dermatological conditions, such as scrofula. Doctors compared sun and sea to meat and wine, for their reinvigorative powers.

Professor Paolo Mantegazza, an apostle of Italian hygiene, noted in 1869 that women "for fear of appearing in the sea otherwise than dolled up by dressmakers, corset-makers and milliners, cover themselves in such thick woollens that

they lose all the benefit the sea can give in its delicious caresses".

From 1865 onwards, bathing-costume fashion was set down precisely: puffed trousers, narrowing at the ankles only, covered by an overgarment with a close-fitting bodice, a belted waist and a short skirt reaching to the knee. The hair was hidden under a large bathing-cap or straw hat, and the feet shod with flat, light slippers.

The same model was proposed by the women's magazine *Novità* in 1872, with slight variations of material and details, including the first use of "marine" braiding, which was to remain a beach-fashion for fifty years until it became a classic, like the collar with a wide square bib behind.

The ever-present bath-robe, to be worn immediately after emerging from the water for drying purposes, was also intended to prevent any exhibition of the body, still considered excessively daring. The robe was comfortable and loose, with wide sleeves and a hood.

By 1876 the overgarment had become less ample, and fell softly onto the trousers, which varied from knee- to ankle-lenght.

Bathing-dress for little girls was enlivened with ribbons and bows. Bathing-slippers were to be "of grey sailcloth lacing above the foot ... the little leather sole, garnished externally with a thin copper plate ... has many small holes to let the water out. The whole is bordered with red woollen ribbon in front and embellished with a knot of the same ribbon".

15.

13. The beaches begin to fill up, even though beachwear is still most chaste in the second half of the 19th century. One could change into a costume with layers of petticoat in improvised cabins made of tenting, or in Oriental-style pavilions.
Carlo Jotti, *Ai bagni*, 1862. Private collection, Lecco.

14. In 1848, lady-bathers are still entering the sea completely dressed.
Engraving, *The Impudent Wave*, by A. Crowquill.

15. The *Princesse* line was to be seen on the beach, as in the case of ordinary dresses. Fashion-plate of 1878. Centro Studi di Storia del Costume, Palazzo Mocenigo, Venice.

16. By the 1870's, bathing-costume skirts had shortened a little, hair was worn under Renaissance-style caps and decoration with blue and white braid began to appear. *La Novità* n. 23, 1872.

16.

Bathing-caps were "of transparent cloth", garnished with crimped pleats or little woollen ribbons. They are flat in front and built up high behind to hold the very long hair then worn, often complicated by hair-pieces.

In the late 1870's bathing-suits followed the characteristics of dress-fashion, especially the unwaisted *princesse* line.

Although ladies appeared on the beach, with its bathing-huts in the form of cabins, wearing *tournures* with long trains, *falbalas* and ostrich-feathers waving on enormous hats, they entered the water in garments of a simpler, more slender cut.

Slippers with Greek lacing, and conch-shaped bonnets completed the beach-costume.

The material most often mentioned in the fashion papers is flannel: white, *écru* or navy blue.

The first wickerwork chairs appeared, with a high baldaquin affording protection against the sun and the salt breezes, especially those of the North Sea.

In 1879, *Margherita* proposed a very original bathing-costume, because the "blouse", hanging down to the knees, almost completely hid the trousers "buttoned at the hips". Another "with short waist", was new because it seemed to be a complete overall, with a fully-visible

pair of trousers. Both these suits could be made up in cloth or wool, while for the straight bath-robe, with hood, white flannel was preferred, or a mysterious "Rubb material"

The 80's did not bring forth many novelties: beach-chairs looked like the insides of carriages and trousers were again hidden under tight waisted blouses with frilled hips. Bathing-caps were shaped like skull-caps, with gathered edges, bath-robes became wider and beach-fashions adopted striped jerseys like those of sailors, or in any case of striped material. Embroidery took the shape of anchors, yachts and ships' steering-wheels.

The last decade of the century was livelier, notable for an excess of ornament and superstructures in the shape of braid, guimping, collars and fringes, and for the "wasp-waist", which involved wearing a corset under the bathing-costume. Larger and larger puffed sleeves were worn, trousers were tighter and the skirt shorter

and bell-shaped. Tle leg-of-mutton sleeves gave rise to the very American invention of the inflatable sleeve, blown up with a bicycle-pump and useful as a lifebelt, mentioned in the *New York World* in August 1895, accompanied by an illustration.

The same line as the full sleeves can be seen in certain bathing-trousers *à la zouave*, sometimes so puffed out as to seem Turkish. The material most used for this purpose is cotton or woollen serge, which, in the case of the younger set, can be cherry-red.

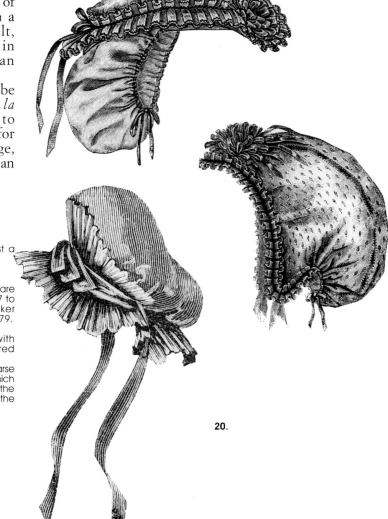

17. Beachwear, costumes and bath-robe against a background of the seaside with its bathing-huts. *Illustrierte Frauen Zeitung* n. 13, 1884.

18. Reading from left to right, the costumes shown are described as white flannel, écru flannel for a girl of 7 to 9 years old, and red flannel. The hodded wicker beach-chair makes its appearance. *Bazar.* Berlin 1879.

19. White flannel or *Rubb* material bath-robe with deep-blue embroidery. The lined hood is gathered round the face with an elastic.
A bathing-suit and jacket. "Can be made up in coarse deep-blue cloth or woollen material. The stockings (which the little girl can go without), remain hidden under the blouse, which is pleated in front with a large yoke; the back, however, is cut *princesse* fashion". *Margherita* n. 31, 1879.

20. Transparent cloth bathing-caps. *La Novità* n. 25, 1876.

20.

22.

23.

21.

21. Among coarse-cloth bathing-shoes, held by footgear, those in natural sailcloth with leather soles, pierced to let the water out, and decorated outside with a brass strip. *Margherita* n. 13, 1899.

22.23. Red serge costume with assymetrical gathered collar, and costume of blue serge and waterproof silk. The lines of the bodice show that a corset is being worn underneath. *Margherita* n. 11, 1897.

24.

Beach-chairs become more complicated and, combined with hangings and bath-robes, give the effect of an encampment.

Headgear consists of a waterproof scarf, knotted over the forehead in Brazilian fashion, or of an oilcloth bathing-cap.

Belts, which may be very wide, are made of rubber. No references can be found to the Liberty style, but there is a Parisian note in some costumes that follow closely the styles worn for the French Can-Can at the Moulin Rouge, with various layers of rustling skirt and naughty black stockings. Bathing-caps are obviously inspired by the Phrygian caps of the French Revolution.

Very often the blouse-like bodices open with a V-neck to show horizontally-striped or herringbone-patterned vests.

There is a renewal, with a will to win eventually, of the "combination", that is to say a one-piece bathing-suit.

The variety of beach shoes and slippers in enormous: polka-dotted, striped, self-coloured, but always with long laces or ribbons.

24. Lifebelt sleeves, according to an American patent. Drawing by Fiora Gandolfi from *New York World*, August 1895.

22

25. Bathing-costume and accessories. The establishment's staircase leading straight into the water is behind.
La Stagione n. 20, 1895.

THE TWENTIETH CENTURY: AN ERA OF SEA-BATHING AND HOLIDAYS

26. In the early years of the 20th century men and chidren bathed in maillots, while ladies kept their dignity, wearing hats and gloves.

TIMID NOVELTIES, REVIVALS AND HYGIENE-MANIA

The beginning of the century disappointed those who put their faith in big changes. In the early years everything went on nearly as before, at least in the field of bathing-costumes, and remained so until the 20's.

Articles in women's magazines about the beneficial effects of sea-bathing had by now become habitual. However, readers were reccomended not to remain more than three minutes in the water, to avoid the "dangerous loss of body-heat". Bathing had become "from the barren sand of a wind-blown shore to the most elegant and smartest establishment, the favourite summer occupation; sometimes a necessity, but always a cool, comfortable and pleasant pastime". There was increased advertising for beaches, which when well-equipped became as famous as the Venice Lido or Rimini. At least those families that could afford it began to make a habit of spending the summer-holidays by the sea for part of the time, and not only in country houses or villas.

There were also more and more articles in the papers of a pseudo-medical nature, extolling the benefits of sun- and sea-bathing.

It was this concept that, penetrating the consciousness of even humble people, led to a revolution in clothes for the seaside, lake, river or pool-side, the idea being to expose as much of one's body to the sun as one could.

There was still a long way to go, and certain illustrations of the period seem to suggest a reactionary movement.

La Mode Illustrée, La Saison and *Le Moniteur de la Mode* for Summer, 1900, present certain quite pratical "combination" models, but they mainly show long 19th century blouses over antiquated-looking trousers, and bath-robes as heavy as Renaissance cassocks.

The materials used are periwinkle-blue serge, "fine red wool" and "striped woollen vests", with a clear preference for blue in all its shades. The repeatedly mentioned serge is simply a diagonally-woven woollen cloth.

The bath-robes shown by *Margherita* in 1901 are red and white flannel of military cut, or more practically-cut embroidered towelling, accompanied by pretty sack-shaped handbags bearing marine motifs.

The lace inserts in the bathing-suits add an elegant and surprising note.

La Stagione of the following year shows a "bathing-shirt" much resembling a nightdress, even down to its white colour. Another novelty if the tartan material used for yet another costume with a flounced tail.

Le Moniteur de la Mode for 1902 shows bathing - and walking-dresses with skirts cut diagonally on the hips, long enough to cover any trousers worn underneath.

Bright colours are more evident, as are bathing-shirts and the waistless "reform", almost "empire" style.

Two issues of *Regina* in 1905 contain sensational articles with photos showing open-air gymnastics performed with ropes and weights- almost a form of aerobics before the letter. The costume worn for this is long combinations, but there are also complete knitted, horizontally-striped body-costumes.

Readers were also told that "we do not breathe with our lungs alone, but with our skin as well, which contains millions of nervous filaments thirsting for light. Sunlight stimulates the life of our tissues". And the conclusion was to expose onself to the sun "in a sensibly succinct costume", while hoping for a return to nature as a step on the road to progress.

"Daughters of the Vikings, blonde Scandinavian girls" with their healthy, statuesque physique, were held up as an example to encourage swimming.

In Anglo-Saxon countries, where bathing was more a sport than a passtime, costumes soon became more simple and practical. In 1905, an Australian swimmer, Miss Annette Kellerman, amazed Paris by crossing the city "via the Seine" in a short sleeved woollen costume with a pair of knee-length shorts, covered by a tiny skirt; a sort of forerunner of the overall that used to be worn under bathing-costumes.

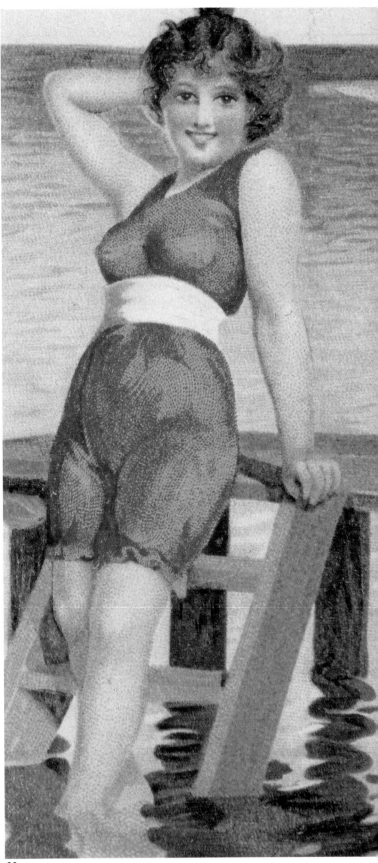

27.28. Scantily-clad, daring "bathing-beauties". Period postcards.

29.

26

Before becoming the acknowledged sportsmodel *Annette Kellerman*, this get-up, worn by Ms. Kellerman on the beaches of Boston in 1920, caused her arrest for indecent exposure. On the beaches of the "Italian marinas", Rimini, Viareggio and the Venice Lido, improvements were being made to the old wooden bathing-establishments built out on piles, and equipped with galleries and numerous staircases leading directly into the water. In the numerous fashion-papers of the time these often appear as a background to the bathing-suits, which starting from 1906 are often tailored in drell.

29. The appropriate yachting-costume is white for ladies and navy-blue for the "sea-dogs".
Period photo, 10 August 1901.

DIFFERING ADVICE
AND OPINIONS

In the same year, the "know-all" journalist of the time suggested that those bound for the seaside should take with them "a little woollen tailor-made, either of light homespun or of flannel; four blouses; a dress of *foulard*, voile or Crêpe de Chine; an embroidered dress of white batiste; a short coat known as amusant which did not reach to the hips; a feather-boa; a lace or painted gauze scarf to wear round the neck or head, and three hats". For beach-wear, "young ladies should not copy low-necked costumes without sleeves, as they would expose themselves to harsh criticism and would certainly not merit the esteem and respect of decent people".

There was a slight decline of interest in the seaside during this period, in the light of hindsight a mere footnote to the history of sea-bathing, but which created some unease at the time.

In 1908, *Regina* mentioned this situation casually: "Although sea-bathing is no longer so extremely fashionable as it was some years ago, having been discredited by those same doctors who no longer attribute to it all the beneficial effects they used to, there are still many people who enjoy it. Some even believe it good for their health, but for many people it is only an excuse, either to get away from town for a month or two ... or to try an make new acquaintances. But whether undertaken for one or the other of these reasons, women and girls are always worried about choosing a bathing-costume that corresponds to all their personal requirements and also has the necessary qualities of an ideal costume".

"A bathing-suit is never a luxury, like other feminine clothes, but must be perfectly cut to fit the figure instead of bundling it up. It must not lose its shape with use, and be of excellent-quality material, so that it does not change its colour. Wool is preferred to cotton, although certain cotton imitations of wool are not to be despised".

30. At Coney Island in 1904 bathers wore costumes with wide collars falling on the shoulders, bordered in white and blue. Underworld Archives, San Francisco.

30.

27

The article continues its precise and detailed advice and opinions: "What must be avoided at all costs is buying ready-made bathing-costumes, which may seem pretty and attractive, but which are always made too economically to be any good!". So whoever wants a "bathing-dress" that will last for more than a season and keep its shape and colour till the end, should buy the material and trimmings and make it up at home, using a good pattern. The most usual colours, "always in fashion", are *bleu marine*, black, red and white.

Of these, the most resistant colour is black " in which you can make very serious-looking costumes which are none the less elegant, decorating them with white or red trimmings of various sizes". In the matter of bathing-costumes, "true elegance consists in simplicity, perfect cut and the best quality material", and therefore there should be no excessive trimmings.

One must be careful of blue, which fades quickly; red is "reserved for children and young girls" and white "becomes transparent in the water" unless it is lined.

There is also clarification about waterproof bathing-caps, "quite fallen out of use" because useless. If the lady immerses herself completely" water gets in all round the rim, filling the cap and making it into a water-bottle in which all the hair is wetted"; otherwise one must be careful not to get the head wet, in which case "a hat giving protection from the sun will be far more useful", and also more evident, to the detriment of the swimmer's agility. But never mind, the important thing is bathing.

31. The sailor-motif - an anchor in this case - was a must. It was embroidered or applied on the wide collar falling on the shoulders.

Germaine
Goldenberg

31.

32. Beachwear, under the protection of hodded chairs, became a little more daring and languorous. C. 1910.
Rippa Bonatti collection.

30

The bathing-costumes suggested consist of "very wide trousers buttoning beneath the knee, and a long blouse held in at the waist by a belt". One-piece costumes are only admissible for girls up the ages of twelve or thirteen.

New fashion trends always come from women magazines: in the same year, La Stagione distinguished, for their originality, three "swimming-suits on the geisha model", with short sleeves and loose cut. Timidly, and hidden under wide bath-robes, close-fitting knitted costumes with black and white stripes still exist, but they are apparently only meant for children.

31

35.

34.

The only novelty in 1910 was *zouave* trousers with braces, worn over the usual blouse.

A greater variety of materials begins to be used for the costumes; not only wool, especially escot and cheviot, but also silks as taffeta and *faille*, satin and velvet, *foulard* and lustre. Cotton is also used, although the fashion-papers insist on advising the use of wool, which being

33. One always leaves the bathing-hut under a bath-robe, to be laid aside only upon entering the water.
Period postcard. Rippa Bonatti collection.

34. Get-up for wear at spas, where Belle Epoque ladies spend smart but curative holidays. 1906.
Ieri Attualità archives.

35. The ideal summer costume for ladies by the seaside or at spas is white cloth, English embroidery, ruched collar, sunshade, large-brimmed hat and long gloves.
Regina, 1905.

36.

heavier, does not stick to tje body when wet. They refuse even to look at knitwear costumes, because "being hardly decent, they would certainly not to be chosen by our readers".

Costumes are always cut close to the figure, with or without cuts in the waist, making them very similar in shape, though not in length, to summer frocks.

Legs are veiled in light-coloured or black stockings, with ankles highlightned by the crossed ribbons of the *espadrilles*.

Bath-robes are of damasked towelling, *ton sur ton* in white or khaki, heavily embroidered or showily "floral".

36. Seaside postcards show decidedly audacious bathers, in daring costumes. 1902. Period postcard, Rippa Bonatti collection.

37. On North Sea beaches, "blondes" go about gaily in clinging costumes. Period postcard, c. 1905. Rippa Bonatti collection.

38. Drawing by Pierre Brissaud. *La Gazette du Bon Ton*, 1919.

37.

38.

To soften the outline of bathing-caps, fringes or "new false curls" are used to make the *coiffure* seem more elegant and coquettish; some women wear a handkerchief on the head, bringing the knot forward to look pretty, while others cover their heads with a *foulard* worn as a bonnet.

There is a great vogue for naughty seaside *trompe-l'-oeil* postcards, which at first sight seem to promise piquant nudities, but which, when the folding element comes down to complete the picture, turn out to be innocent, amusing deceptions.

Throughout the first years of the century people continue to frequent spas, which in Europe are places for select, luxury holidays. Water-cures compete with the sea, attracting a growing number of clients.

Smart receptions in the *villes d'eaux*, as

they are known in France, take place at the Casino, the racecourse, at garden-parties and in the *salons* of private villas and hotels.

Ladies go to Salsomaggiore, Italian politicians to Fiuggi, everyone to Montecatini, and anaemic girls to Aix-les-Bains and Bagnol-les-Bains. And elegant ladies converge on many other European spas, naturally with their husbands, and surrounded by an escort of little daughters and ladies' maids.

The style of dress for these occasions is always very summery and sparkling, as suggested by the canons of taste of the vaporous Belle Epoque, and differs little from clothes for the seaside, with changes of costume according to the occupation of the wearer and the time of day. Dresses of linen or linon, preferably white (that being thought the non-colour suitable for summer) are always embroidered in English or Irish point, and *ruches*, flounces and *jabots* are superimposed to form corollas. Thus titivated, the lady goes forth to the *buvette* for her first morning glass of curative water. But for the inevitable afternoon therapeutic appointment (another glass of water), she wears a white tailor-made. The long, simple "hobble-skirt" was at this period decorated with incrustations of flowers or other motifs in Irish lace, and the linon blouse with hemstitching, striped with *entre-deux* or Irish lace. The jacket, or *petit paletot* that completed the get-up had, according to *Les Modes*, to be a masterpiece of complicated embroidery, twisting among hemstitching and showy *guipures*: as if this were not enough, emphasized as well with silk trimming.

This elegant ensemble was topped off with a little handbag, a very pale cupola sunshade and a hat covered in flowers, feathers and ribbons, all combining to pretect the transparent opalescence of the beautiful wearer.

"Against the sun and its fierceness, against the reflections from the sea and the street, against moonlight which, as you know, is harmful to delicate complexions" the hygienist advises the use of veils, which had been worn for decades with casual elegance by very *chic* and lanky Englishwomen.

39. The Vittoria chain-stores advertise new bathing-costumes models on knitted wool, the figure is hidden under capes of white towelling. Bathing-slippers are not forgotten.
Raccolta Stampe Bertarelli, Milan. Photo Saporetti.

40. Shot-taffeta bathing-costume, changing shades like reflections from the sea. Drawing by George Barbier, 1913

BEACH FASHIONS

In 1911, *L'Onda del Lido* noticed the appearance on the beach of a little *jupe culotte*: "the brown petticoat, blown about by the wind, showed elegant drawers with brown and white stripes, making a triumph of the costume".

This was the time of Thomas Mann's *Death in Venice*, published in 1912. Who can forget the reconstruction of the beach and costumes ordered by Luchino Visconti from Tirelli for the film of that title?

Although in Italy emphasis was still upon models increasingly similar to ordinary dresses, with incorporated shorts that dared to call themselves the height of novelty, France turned to classical Greek and Roman models, or to ancient Persian styles, with variously draped cloaks. Jean Silvère was telling women on the beach to think of Isadora Duncan, to imitate her and not deprive men of the sight of "the brilliant whiteness of your slender legs"; they wore canvas cothurni on their feet and light turbans or wide Greek hats on their heads.

There was a clear trend for bathing-suits to adhere closer to the body, a trend underlined and prettified by such talented designers as Barbier.

36

42.

41.43. A panorama of seaside attitudes: some are plunging in, some test the water with a doubting toe, others check their own elegance and still others swim like Undines, dressed according to a fashion that calls for bathing garments of classical cut.
Drawing by Brissaud, 1913.

38

44.

45.

46.

Sports bathing-caps, very like those worn for the Olympics to-day, made their first appearance.

Until 1914, the belt tended to descend onto the hips, and this was true of bathing-costumes also.

As regards materials, mention is made of cretonne or percale, either striped or floral, but knitwear was becoming more to the fore, and by 1915 it had reached the cover of *La Vie Parisienne*, as well as appearing in tradesmen's catalogues, and was available in three sizes. It was very similar for men and women, except that for the latter it consisted of "combinations and blouse", garnished with "white braid".

Erté, the famous costumier and fashion-designer, showed the extent of his inventive powers by producing models for beachwear that were divinely theatrical. Drawing inspiration for everything from mythology to folklore, while fully understanding the female form, which he almost overdressed, he eroticized women by exposing unusual areas of their skin.

The names of his creations, Perle de l'Océan, Sirène Captive, Fille de Neptune, Caresse des Flots and Pêche Miraculeuse explain his spirit and achievements.

47.

48.

39

49.

But blouses and trousers did not disappear; they even enjoyed a justifiable vogue during the war.

Menawhile belts were moving up or down, completely undecided as to where to go but refusing to stay in the right place.

There were no great changes of outline, but the beginnings of a new attitude towards sunbathing.

A Venetian journalist, writing under the pseudonym of *Passepartout* in the *Rivista Balneare* in 1919, stressed the fact that "while in past years lovely ladies tried to mitigate the sun's violence with veils and wide-brimmed hats, this year they have discarded all forms of protection - shoulders and arms, even in the most reluctant cases, show signs of suntan".

44. 49. Famous designer Erté improvises, for summer 1915, a series of bathing-suits reflecting his preference for theatrical costume.

THE SUPER-ELEGANT TWENTIES

51.

EXOTIC BEACH-HUTS
AND SEASIDE DANCE-FLOORS

The creative and formal elegance characteristic of the 20's also affected the bathing-dress; when it did not resemble evening-dress in its refinement and luxury, it was always pleasant and never vulgar.

Woollen jersey had won the fight on all fronts, trousers had been shortened to mid-thigh, and blouses, with square or crew necklines, reached to the groin. Knotted scarves and *foulards* hid the hair, replaced by rubber bathing-caps when in the water.

Bath-robes were ample and round like cloaks, or in the form of shawls.

Beaches were studded with parasols, sometimes completed with a curious type of desert-tent, to the detriment of the ever-more attractive beach-huts.

The first dance-floors, the famous *"rotonde sul mare"*, where one "danced, danced to the heady tunes of the fox-trot" and practised other new American dances, were opened in this period. From the "New World" came also the revised version of the *Annette Kellerman* bathing-suit: a black knitwear, sleeveless costume with large shoulder-straps and a round neckline on the back, which was chosen as official outfit for the female swimmer-team at the 1928 Amsterdam Olympic games.

50. An absolutely anticipatory futuristic design concludes the parade of 1910's bathing-costumes.

51. Erté has created a bathing-costume made of taffeta ribbons, shading from sunburst-yellow into deepest blue, and held in place with silk threads. The cap is yellow and the slippers of blue cloth.

42

52.

One entered the sea on white wooden pedalos with two elements, and learnt to swim.

Depero, Thayaht and Balla designed bathing-suits of futuristic cut with a bold juxtaposition of colours that produced a dynamic composition.

Despite undoubted progress on the road to emancipation, bigoted moralists warned against the "snares of taffeta "which, once wetted, adhered scandalously to the body; however

52. Fashion-designer Simeon created in 1921 a costume for swimming-lessons, made of black silk with printed borders and a shawl bath-robe to match. *La Gazette du Bon Ton, 1921.*

53. Sailor-inspired beach-suit in white-and-blue-striped silk. Drawing by Brissaud. *La Gazette du Bon Ton, 1920.*

54.

carefully and quickly one covered this up in a bath-robe, "something can always be perceived by the vigilant eye of a malicious public on the look-out for such things".

For the moment, the belt had slipped down to the hips. The line was straight, the little skirt short and flounced.

There was a little simple geometrical or nature-inspired decoration on the bodice. Drawers were still worn underneath, but they could hardly be seen.

The *Rinascente* chain-store catalogue for Summer, 1925, presents a series of two-piece costumes, blouse and shorts, in knitwear, cretonne, shiny silk, and alpaca.

54. A collection of bathing-costumes and bath-robes from a sales-catalogue. *Abiti estivi,* 1925.

Colours are "navy, coral, black, Nattier and red with trims". The bath-robes are white, peach, yellow and brick-red. There are rubber belts, "canvas bathing-shoes with rope-soles" or sponge-rubber linings; rubber head-scarves; "smooth" bathing-caps and those decorated with flower or fancy motifs; white piqué cloche or American-style caps (like Popeye's, who had just made his appearance).

Meanwhile, shivers of terror ran along the beaches without however spoiling the fun; sharks had been seen in the calm waters of our seas, and there had even been a serious accident at Varazze, so that "no bather enters the sea without a certain

feeling of horror at the thought of Jonah's fate ... were it not for a question of appearances, they would all go in armed to the teeth. In any case, sharks or not, the season is drawing to a close and many people are preparing to go home bearing obvious signs of their time by the sea: necks, arms and chests well tanned by the sun, and cocoa-coloured faces imitating Aida's. All this so that people should know they've been at the seaside".

How true those words still ring to-day!

55. A young lady, in "beach-clothes" of taffeta and slippers laced slave-fashion, on the sand in front of the "Excelsior". Venice Lido, 1924. *Ieri Attualità* archives.

56.

and the "one-piece knitted wool for swimming".

Coco Chanel had a great influence on the evolution of bathing-costumes: she designed those worn in Diaghilev's ballet *Le Train Bleu,* staged at the Théâtre des Champs Elysées in 1925. They were soft and clinging without being vulgar: the material, striped only at the lower edges of blouse and shorts, seems to have been made of heavyish knitted wool, occasionally *bouclé.* The style was exactly the same for both men and women dancers: a foretaste of unisex fashion.

56. An advertisement for the *Rinascente* chain-stores shows a most elegant costume. Early 20's. *Raccolta Stampe Bertarelli,* Milan. Photo Saporetti.

57. Brilliant designer Thayaht, upholder of "futurist" ideology, invented a bathing-suit with a neckline of entwined shoulder-straps. *La Gazette du Bon Ton,* 1921.

58. For 20's summer seasons, *Au Grand Frédéric* suggests "combinations" of singlets and shorts for beach and bathing elegance. *Deauville* made.

HIGH FASHION'S CONTRIBUTION

Then French high-fashion turned to designing bathing-suits, like the delicious ones shown in 1925 on *Fémina,* created by Jeanne Lanvin: "a tunic of cherry-red jersey over very short shorts of the same material, decorated with black pastilles", those of Jeanne Patou "black marocain with wavy green incrustations" or Jane Régny's "black jersey trimmed in white with two little pockets under the belt".

Advice was given to personalize one's bath-robe, be it close-fitting or flounced like a wide skirt, with a monogram.

The sporting bathing-cap gave "the face, freed from all artifice, an incredible expressivity".

The accent was always on simplicity.

Italian models, too, though not signed by their designers, were very refined; of various silks for the check bodice, the light-coloured blouse contrasting with dark shorts, the transverse placing of colours and the alternation of upper and lower quarterings.

There was a clear distinction between "beach-costume" of knitted silk "strangely disposed, the bodice higher on one side and a gathered skirt with big festoons",

57.

46

Fashion-papers were saying that sunbathing-mania was due to the growing importance of seaside holidays in people's lives. In 1929, *Fémina* was quite clear about this: "It is obligatory to spend one month of the year roasting on the sand, and every girl who follows the fashion would be dishonoured if she didn't come back at the end of the summer with a magnificent white-coffee, or at least pale-chocolate tan. As coquettishness never loses its sway, bathing-costumes have been revised, varied and studied in such a way that the greatest possible fantasy be devoted to these little pieces of cloth".

59.

Bathing-suits were also being worn beside the pools of spas, in the gardens of town villas, those of hill-resorts and even in the high mountains.

A natural look was recommended: networks of gilt links, Roman-draped mantles held at the shoulder with a gilt brooch, or any other eccentricity, was in bad taste.

Jean Patou set the example of measure and tact, with his charming, vivacious costumes: "his straight, soft silk or flowered cloth cloaks are accompanied by a large bag of the same material and a wide, curly-brimmed straw hat". The bathing-suit has a little flat skirt that does away with the "unseemly realistic effects of knitwear".

Hermès, too, is quoted as an example of refined simplicity, relieved by incrusted motifs in bright colours. Elsa Schiaparelli has waterproof taffeta under a woollen black-and-white striped *burnous* with matching beret.

One must avoid silk bathing-suits and belts with large bows; at the most, one may pull the waist in with a fancy scarf making a wide belt.

The bathing-costume is, of course, accompained by many accessories: expecially big exotic straw hats, floppy panamas, and a towel in the same material as the bath-robe or cloak to be laid on the beach in order to avoid the horrible look of a fish ready for frying produced by a wet costume in contact with the sand. Then come the tent, the skirt, to be worn over the bathing-suit, the matching cloth or embroidered straw bag with its little mirror, each day reflecting a more sunburnt appearance, and finally the short-handled flat sunshade with its obviously Chineese decoration.

59.-61. For summer 1925, Mateldi, the famous fashion-illustrator, created a collection of knitwear, knitted silk and waterproof taffeta bathing-costumes: Mexican-inspired pyjamas, peplos with floral embroideries and padded-taffeta applications, contrasting colour woollen trimmings for sports-costumes, a hooded taffeta dress with cape sleeves and tassels, and a striped knitwear bathing-suit beautified by waterproof taffeta pleated frills. *Lidel*, 1925.

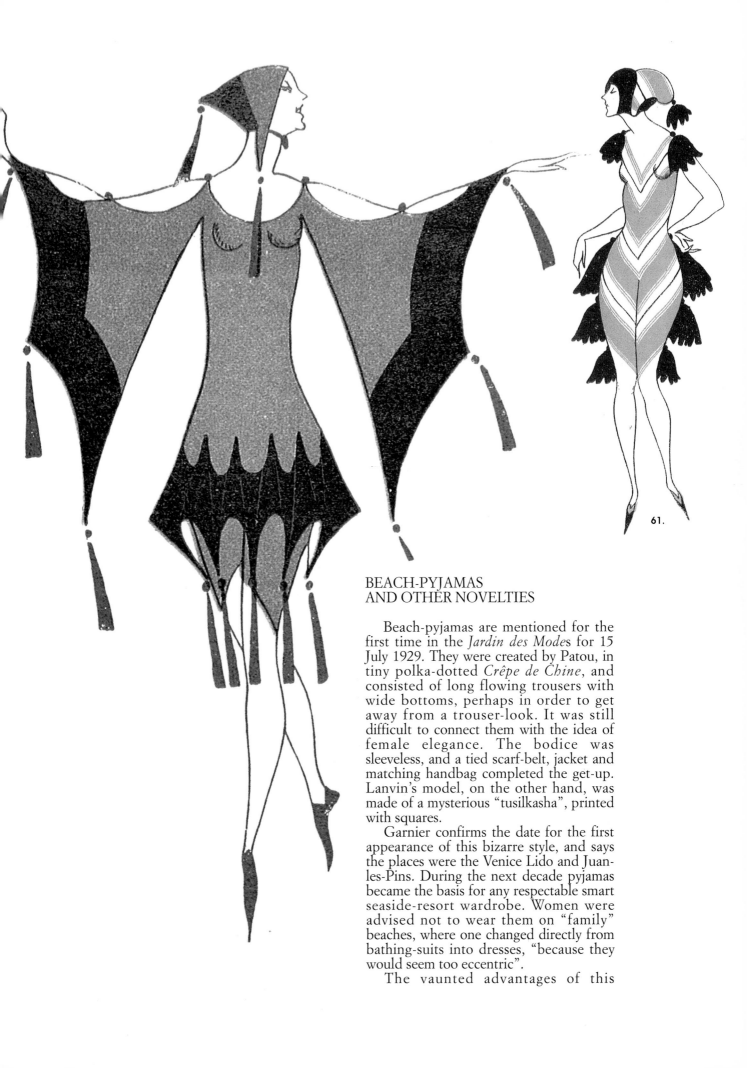

61.

BEACH-PYJAMAS
AND OTHER NOVELTIES

Beach-pyjamas are mentioned for the
first time in the *Jardin des Mode*s for 15
July 1929. They were created by Patou, in
tiny polka-dotted *Crêpe de Chine*, and
consisted of long flowing trousers with
wide bottoms, perhaps in order to get
away from a trouser-look. It was still
difficult to connect them with the idea of
female elegance. The bodice was
sleeveless, and a tied scarf-belt, jacket and
matching handbag completed the get-up.
Lanvin's model, on the other hand, was
made of a mysterious "tusilkasha", printed
with squares.

Garnier confirms the date for the first
appearance of this bizarre style, and says
the places were the Venice Lido and Juan-
les-Pins. During the next decade pyjamas
became the basis for any respectable smart
seaside-resort wardrobe. Women were
advised not to wear them on "family"
beaches, where one changed directly from
bathing-suits into dresses, "because they
would seem too eccentric".

The vaunted advantages of this

62. At the Venice Lido, you leave the Hotel Excelsior and walk along the sunny beach to lunch at the Taverna in bath-robes or Pyjamas. Jane Régny. *Femina*, 1925.

63.64. Pyjamas are the smartest beach-wear of the late 20's. They are in three pieces - trousers, blouse and long, flowing ja-cket and are designed by all the leading French houses: Lucien Lelong, Jean Patou, Worth and Marie Nowitzky. *Fémina*, 1925.

costume were numerous: "it covers the bathing-suit, so that one can remain on the beach without dressing again; it does not require expensive material, as it is usually made of silk, tussore, cretonne, cotton cloth, *fil à fil* woollen muslin, towelling, silk crepe or self-coloured shantung". Velvet was reserved for very smart occasions.

Although only suitable for tall, slim women, everyone wore pyjamas, even "little fatties" who, when they added a cloche hat or a wide-brimmed straw, looked just like so many mushrooms.

All women wore their hair short, blown by the wind or protected by Chinese rice-workers hats, or head-scarves tied "peasant-wise", with the forehead completely covered and a knot at the back or side; eyes were bright with kohl.

1929 brought another novelty: the "Canadian" costume, made of a long sweater and a culotte. A peccary belt threaded through loops emphasized the low waistline.

Noi e il Mondo for August 1929 had a really original cover, on which a white costume with a short skirt cut into symmetrical points, announced the long article inside, dealing with the beach, which tried to analyse the reason for seaside-mania. The reader "seeing bathing-suits that no longer covered anything" would end by realizing that "the world is very sick, because it has lost the idea of goodness and taste". On the positive side, "all beach-society, despite some people's inveterate weaknesses, is convinced of the need to spend at least a month gaily and quietly", and that this cannot be enjoyed "elsewhere than at the seaside, where the sunshine attenuates the perfidious instincts of human progeny". So that sun is seen as a good shepherd, converting the souls of the perverse.

L'Illustrazione d'Italia had an article by Corrado Rossi, its special correspondent at Rimini, making good-natured fun of "certain delicious little costumes of sackcloth, without shoulder-straps, which won cries of unconditional admiration from all the ladies", in contrast to an antiquated eccentric costume of orange velvet that had been worn for two years running by an old English lady.

63.

64.

65. Elegant beach ensembles designed by French fashion-leaders: Worth, Lelong, Lanvin and Schiaparelli, who began her career in that year. *Le Jardin des Modes*, July 1929.

THE SPECIAL SEDUCTION
OF THE THIRTIES

SILK AND TAFFETA FOR THE SUN, STRICT KNITWEAR FOR THE SEA

The 30's, less crazy but equally attractive, displayed the Italian line in *Lidel*, the leading Fascist review, which drove its readers on with cries of "To the sea, to the sea!", saying that the changing blue background of the waters made women look more beautiful than in the grey of cities. Seaside life provided opportunities for a thousand elegances and a thousand new ways of appearing pretty. There one could even try to be original without seeming shameless.

For swimming, paddling or pedalo-trips, it was better to stick to brand-name woollen costumes, preferably in dark shades: "at the back, necklines drop to the belt, while, in compensation, they rise to the neck in front. For ease in swimming, costumes are completely masculinized, but still two-piece, a complete blouse and a pair of clinging shorts held up with a rubber belt".

For long hours spent lying in the sun on the sand, there are much more elegant jersey, taffeta and even silk costumes in light shades and of far more feminine cut, including pretty little costumes, in silk or linen, with little wide sailor-collared blouses and blue-and-white shorts.

Photos of the time show costumes with the male fatures and naked torso of Mussolini printed on the front. Even in the water you couldn't get away from Fascism.

66. Fashionable bath-robes are long, cut like an evening coat and made of printed sponge-chenille. *Le Jardin des Modes*, June 1931.

and bag in white towelling with black balls and a red border over a red woollen bathing-suit decorated with the same black balls, the other, of sailor-inspiration, a dark blue thick-silk pyjama, a blue-and-white striped jersey and a little cap with a pompom.

67.

67. One refinement of beach-fashion is the Valaguzza belt with its waterproof compartment to hold cigarettes and make-up requisites. *Lidel,* 19 June 1931.

68. The 30's witnessed an outbreak of hunger for holidays, and women's magazines ran articles on knitting bathing-costumes for women, too. *Lidel,* June 1931.

69. An advertisement by Jantzen, the renowned bathing-costume manifacturer, published on *Les Jardin des Modes,* June 1931.

Readers were told that everywhere now "the pyjama triumphs, and dress-designers' fancies run riot trying to create original ones, often inspired by classic costumes. They can be found in every shape, shade and material, white crepe satin, black velvet, flowered or polka-dot crêpe de Chine, with long jackets down to the knee, little Mexican boleros, svelte sleeveless jackets; worn with *foulards,* scarves, belts, lace; with the shirt inside or outside the trousers and with wide trousers forming almost a skirt. They dress one admirably, while leaving complete freedom of movement. Even ladies reluctant to follow the fashion have been convinced that a dressing-gown, which threatens to open at any moment and under which one must remain dressed, could not be more comfortable".

Even beach-hats came in for some unusual changes. Very wide clothes of satin, organdi and embroidered linen coexist with little bonnets leaving the forehead bare and covering the nape, and bonnets of all shapes in straw, silk, chenille or wool "almost always matching the shade of the costume or pyjamas".

Fashion-news for 1931 mentions two beach-outfits; one, a coordinated jacket

68.

Les costumes de bain "Jantzen" assurent cette élégance si nécessaire au bord de la mer. La beauté d'un costume de natation réside avant tout dans sa coupe; non pas seulement dans la façon dont il moule le corps avant d'avoir été mouillé, mais après avoir été plusieurs fois à l'épreuve de l'eau.

Les coloris joyeux, la nouveauté des modèles, la manière dont s'ajustent les costumes "Jantzen" sont les raisons véritables de leur supériorité et de la préférence que les baigneurs leur témoignent. Vous trouverez les "Jantzen" dans toutes les meilleures maisons.

Exigez sur votre maillot la plongeuse rouge comme marque de garantie.

55

69.

SOME EXCELLENT ACCESSORIES
FOR AN ADEGUATE WARDROBE

When discussing the little details that decide the elegance of a fascinating woman with a distinct personality, one finds that she chooses from the fashion of the day "the most refined and at the same time simpliest thing, that she knows how to adapt for any time and place". The conclusion is that nobody can do without a "Valaguzza belt".This accessory is made of soft wool in the most fashionable shades. It is shrink-proof and closed with an artistic metal buckle, delicately enamelled and lacquered in various colours with designs inspired by the best modern taste. It also contains a hidden treasure, for inside it is a complete make-up set, with mirror, rouge, lipstick and powder or cigarettes. "Even if the sea is rough, water cannot get into the

56

mysterious little buckle, and the lovely lady can repair damage caused by spume and wind, making her face up even while still in the sea, like an undine, on the beach or on board ship. Her swimming-companion can hand her a cigarette with a gallant gesture, for thanks to the miraculous belt it will be intact and dry".

In an amusing article, *Lidel* describes the things one must not forget when going to the seaside; at least two costumes, one simple, slim one for bathing, and a showier two-coloured one for shipboard; at least three pyjamas, one white, easily washed and not ostentatious, one more original of sailor-cut, made of cotton or light wool, and a rather sumptuous silk one.

"Be clever enough" it adds "to have them made in separate parts, so that you can mix them, and kid yourself that you've six at least".

72.

You also need two rubber bathing-caps, a pair of rubber shoes in addition to sandals, at least a pair of "those famous magic waterproof belts", a thick cloth hat and a straw one. As for berets, the Fascist review is peremptory: "not Basque berets, please, for Spain is out of fashion now that it has gone mad". Finally you need a comfortable cretonne or printed crepe jacket to wear over the costume, a hold-all bag, sunshades and "walnut oil" to protect your skin from the sun.

70. Along with pyjamas, of pink crepe in this case, which it is smart to wear over the swimsuit, there is also a fashion for swimming-pools with springboards, built even by the sea itself in elegant bathing-resorts.
Fémina, July 1930.

71.72. Seaside elegance for the beach and all other times was illustrated in the 30's by Gruau.
Lidel, July 1932, June 1934.

58

THE BATHER'S PSYCHOLOGY, OR HUMANITY LAID BARE

All papers, not only those written for women, abound in colourful articles about beach-life and its psychological background.

It seems that "humanity laid bare is much more mysterious that humanity clad, and that the more clothes are removed the more the mystery deepens. On land, with the daily disguise of clothing, one can tell a goddess from a shopgirl, but in the water or on the beach things are much more difficult. The moral?: "clothes make the woman". Furthermore, "usually, in daily life, women try and always succeed in finding devices to cheat over the topography of their figures, while in the sea they are obliged to confess their

73. Beach Pyjamas illustrated by Gruau. *Lidel*, 15 June 1931.

73.

59

shortcomings".

Clever dressmakers can find ways of cheating even at the seaside, but these are little shifts, or which not too much reliance should be placed. "They cannot be compared with the surprises that a woman can spring with her figure when in ordinary clothes". In conclusion, it is as well to beware of a woman who won't wear a bathing-dress, because she must have some grave fault to hide.

Some people, however, affirm the contrary, and say that a woman clothed is much more fascinating than a naked one, agreeing with Socrates, who said that if a naked woman could be seen as a masterpiece, once dressed she would an undiscovered masterpiece, and therefore more seductive: for in every man there lurks the intrepid spirit of an explorer.

HOLIDAYS UNDER FASCISM

The number of fashionable beaches increased all over Italy. Already in the 20's, the rocky coast of Istria and the Dalmatian islands, that had become Italian at the end of the first world war, were becoming smart as well. The big hotels of Abbazia and the pine-forests round the inlets of Lussino Island, site of the Trieste shipowners' villas, were attracting a select clientele. The rocks, pines and exclusive hotel of Brioni, pearl of the Adriatic - also frequented by a Middle European public - were scenes of eccentricities, though only of a sporting nature.

Rome had six beaches: two popular ones (Ladispoli and Fiumicino) where Sunday trains poured out floods of people from humble homes, courtyards, alleys and tenements; then there was the port of Anzio, a classic Roman beach frequented by the lowest ranks of the nobility and the highest of the bourgeoise - politicians, industrialists and professional men; lower middle-class Ostia, Fregene, elegant and snobbish; and finally Santa Marinella with its luxury patriarchal villas.

74. Knitted-wool bathing-costumes. *Mani di fata*, June 1933.

75. Billboards advertising Abbazia, the fashionable summer resort that during the '30s became the destination of elegant and sportive holydays. *Lidel*, June 1934.

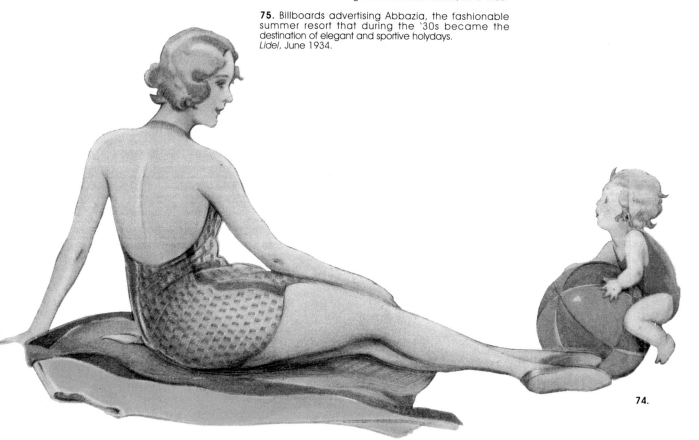

74.

R.GRUAU
33

Then there were Bellaria and Riccione, the latter having been chosen for a decade by Mussolini's family for its summer abode, which meant that Italian Fascist ardour promoted all the Romagna beaches to the rank of tourist attractions.

The crowds of people, mainly women, on the beach at Riccione were partly due to the wish to see the Duce (with a capital D) appear in a bathing-suit. Apparently there would then be scenes of unbridled enthusiasm. The parade of beach-fashion and exhibitionism was animated by the hope that "He" would at least glance in one's direction. We hear that a whole fleet of pedalos, crewed by women longing for a sight of Mussolini's bare chest, converged and foundered on the seashore. But not all of them knew that, when he sailed away on his launch, it was to meet his lady-friend, dressed in a bathing-suit and long white dressing-gown, waiting on a pedalo some hundred yards off Rimini beach.

The Italians also frequented the Tuscan coast, Marina di Pisa, Alassio, Positano and Posillipo, as well as Capri, Ischia and Procida, mainly sought after by the Neapolitans.

Speaking of Positano at that time, the well-known Italian journalist Gaetano Afeltra remembers with affection that: "the bathers came out of the boarding-houses, the men in silk pyjamas and rope-soled shoes, the women in large towelling bath-robes, brightly coloured over their costumes. The grand parade took place on the dance-floor of the bathing-establishment, where the bath-robed ladies stopped a moment to refresh themselves before entering their bathing-huts. Most of the men never went in the water; they had come there for a rest, and they talked, read the papers, at the most sat in a deck-chair in the shade on the beach. Our girl-friends came down later, hot and bothered, and went into their huts, from which they emerged resplendent, wearing blue, white or green bathing-caps".

These beauties would step into the water, and after getting used to the temperature by sprinkling themselves, would make the sign of the cross, plunge in and begin to swim.

But they didn't only swim in the sea; it had become fashionable to bathe in lakes and even rivers, too.

77.

Pretentious establishments sprang up there too, with luxury bathing-huts, circular dance-floors restaurants, "toboggans", springboards and swings. It was just like the sea, except that, when swimming, one found one's mouth full of sweetish, insipid water.

The Fascist dictatorship strung along the coasts of the peninsula "marine colonies" for children and young boys, who arrived there in squadrons to improve their physical and psychical health during the holidays. Their stay was organized on quasi-military lines, punctuated by "noble rites and severe discipline which augur well for the future" (*La Lettura*, 1931).

76.77. Knitted-wool bathing-costumes from the Italian firm *Dazza;* they were more daring and tended towards the "two-piece". Drawings by René Gruau.
Lidel, May 1933.

MORE SUN MEANS BETTER HEALTH

Bathing-suits had undergone a slow and almost imperceptible change. It Italy too there were followers of naturist ideas, who attacked "sun-suits" with their scissors, so that ultra-violet rays - the danger from which was still unknown - could confer maximum benefit.

Women were advised to personalize their usually self-coloured costumes with some original embroidery, for which the fashion-papers provided patterns. Jersey bathing-suits seemed to soften the outlines of the body, while facilitating movements of the shoulders, arms and legs. Deep neck-openings at the back made for good suntan.

The most famous trade-mark was

Jantzen, recognizable from the little outline of a woman swimmer embroidered on the drawers.

Kestos and Atlante, two other manufacturers, made one-piece suits of stretchable knitwear with plunging necklines "for sunbathing", that "enabled the maximum exposure of the back while remaining decent".

Spalding made the two-piece *Canadien*, a short tunic and little square shorts, a simple and classic "swimsuit", and the *American*, with a chaste skirtlet.

Tunmer not only made costumes, but also accessories such as rubber bathing-caps painted with wavelets, light swimming-sandals or painted clogs for walking on the burning sand.

In 1932, the shorts came completely away from the bodice, leaving the midriff uncovered; or remained attached at the belt with a little triangular strip of material "leaving exposed to air and sun all of our body that we can expose without offending chastity and good taste".

The new costumes stick to the body like a second skin; a little skirt hangs down to protect decorum. Pyjamas are replaced by *robes maillot*, completed by skirts draped round the body, little jackets or boleros.

In 1933 *Lidel* insists on the healthful effects of sunshine-cures, noting that "a more intensive beach-life, to which all may now aspire without distinctions of social position, and the new, healthy habit of cruises, are undoubtedly preparing a strong generation, with increased resistance and capable of a noteworthy demographic improvement". This reads more like an advertisement for a shipping-line than a scientifically provable fact.

The costume-novelty for the year is hand-knitted, with close stitches forming vertical ribs; instructions for knitters are provided.

65

78. The cover of Vogue showed a foretaste of the 70's monokini. Drawing by Lepape. *Vogue*, July 1934.

79. Beach get-up made up by a corset and a wide skirt (worn over shorts in the same material), and topped off by sailor-style decorative buttons. *Jardin des Modes*, June 1936.

79.

One could also knit a kind of triangular handkerchief, held in at the collar and knotted at the waist, leaving the back completely bare. It could be worn with shorts, pyjama trousers or the long straight ones, that were beginning to appear in smart wardrobes. The same result could also be had by knotting an ordinary *foulard* in the required way.

The refined and clever readership of *Vogue* must have been shocked by its cover for July '34; designed by Lepape, Paul Poiret's stylist, it showed a sunburnt young woman of vaguely androgynous appearance, surrounded by seashells and starfish, and wearing nothing but a pair of white shorts. To understand the boldness of this, one has only to think what a scandal it would still have caused thirty years later.

Inside the review, the article on beach-fashion contained nothing shocking; instead, there were very elegant models by Olga Rosen (a pleated cape transformable into a skirt) and by Heim: "it's no longer necessary for very feminine women to look like *manqué* boys. Heim has drawn inspiration from the South Seas for the pareo covering the hips, completed by a

brassiere attached to the shoulders by a ribbon".

The writer explains all the advantages of Tahitian costume: "There can be nothing prettier than a pareo. Its shape? That of the body. Its shades? Those of the sky, the sea, the hibiscus-flower, the moonfish and the firebird. Not is there anything more decent than a pareo; nothing more undressed, nothing plainer and nothing more select. Do you have good legs? Then wear it half way down the thigh. Do you prefer to hide them? Then let it fall down to the feet. It frees your breast and hides it, bares it and flattens it, holds it up and abandons it". Once out of the sea, an elegant woman can keep her bathing-suit on, draping herself in a square of matching cotton, or can put on a smock and a beret to give herself the air of a comic little sailor.

Two original cloaks were also shown, one "shaped like a tent, the other of a burnous type, both big enough for one to be able to undress under them as safely as in a bathing-hut".

81.

THE PERPLEXITIES
OF A HARDENED CYNIC

The transformation of beaches into high concentrations of masses of people aroused perplexity in public opinion and exaggerated reports by journalists, eager to condemn the latest fashion.

Someone writing under the name of Dardano was inveighing in *La Lettura* of 1935: "To my mind, beaches, with their pieces of human meat roasting in the sun's slow fire, the sea-salt that adds flavour and the rough, absorbent sand, have always evoked the idea of a roast-meat shop. Sometimes, moving among those cooked limbs, mostly those of shapely, tender girls, I've had the mouth-watering idea of stopping at a beach-hut and asking, as in a fried-food shop and pointing at an attractive shoulder: "Can I have half a pound of that, please?".

It would be far easier to work out the statistics for the numbers of people on the beaches by using a pair of scales: thirty

80. Jantzen's models for summer 1939 were presented in the following colours: black, Marine, Brasil, garnet, Rio red, Bermuda green, Capri blue and platinum-grey. *Raccolta Stampe Bertarelli,* Milan. Photo Saporetti.

81.82 French fashion-houses included beach elegance in their dress-collections. Printed linen capes to wear over the costume and exotically-inspired pareos by Jacques Heim. *Le Jardin des Modes,* July 1936, June 1936.

82.

tons of meat at Rimini, forty tons at Deauville".

"Human limbs", continues our journalist, who has decidedly cannibalistic tendencies, "are thrown onto the beaches like splendid quarters of meat in the market; the burning sun highlights the ribs, loins, topsides and fillets ... which move indifferently from land to water, becoming boiled beef in the process".

Next he wittily attacks the clothes worn: "Our parents' costumes were made for baths in which the sea played an aquatic role, and the body was still the material envelope to the soul, and not flabby meat. One went to the beach then for long immersion in the water. Those costumes were still based on town-clothes and were whole get-ups, of three or four different garments. Women immerged themselves dressed as it were for a gala evening or a funeral, handbags on their wrists and, in the handbag, a handkerchief to blow one's nose on, whereas to-day, alas, it gets blown in the water with the

help of the fingers. When they emerged from the waves, tottering on the pebbles, they covered themselves in monk-like bath-robes, with enormous penitents' cowls on their heads, concealing every millimitre of their skin from the sun. To-day's costumes are quite another thing; made to show the body off, they could be comfortably be made out of the material of a pair of socks".

The mysterious Dardano ends his leader with an eulogy of "the edges of the beach, with the desert-like outlines of the tents put up for the children's colony, sanatoria, rest-homes that dot the sand", where you can come accross Sisters of Mercy with their large, winged coifs prudishly raising their skirts a little way and gradually immerging "their virginal legs in the sea"; where "humble people take the sun" in undervests and singlets, their trousers rolled up to the knee and a knotted handkerchief on their heads. Although by now it is usual to expose part of the midriff to the sun, it is certain that

the belly and especially the navel are still kept out of sight.

During those years Schiaparelli launched amusing bicoloured canvas hats, like the little boats made out of newspaper worn by bricklayers.

In 1937, *Dea*, an Italian review that had taken *Lidel*'s place, stated that good old walnut oil was no longer used, but was replaced by creams and jellies. Costumes were made of elasticized silk, which "contained and conformed" the body like a sheath, and it was becoming increasingly usual to cover the bust with a simple brassiere.

Sun-suits had clinging décolleté bodices and short pleated skirts with fringes and bows.

To be perfectly equipped, *Grazia* suggested in 1939 that the suitcase should contain "two good bathing-suits, two sun-suits, short and long trousers, and a few blouses, two simple cloth or rayon frocks, a stunning but inexpensive evening-dress, two pairs of sandals, a big hat and a bottle of suntan oil".

83. Two-piece hand-knitted costume. The brassiere strap goes round the neck so as to leave the back as bare as possible. *Le Jardin des Modes*, July 1936.

84. Two-piece beach-suit, tartan sunsuit with puffed shorts and long tunic of white piqué fastened by a zip. *Grazia*, 1 June 1939.

85. Rompers are fashionable wear for sunbathing. *Grazia*, May 1939.

FLOWERS AND COLOURS

Elasticized costumes were destined to become ever more popular because "being completely clinging, they support and modify the lines of the body". They were made by adding elastic filaments to the woven fabric, and these filaments illuminated the material and sheathed the body like close-fitting armour. Often the costumes had beautiful designs and unusual colours.

"Covering bathing-costumes with the most fanciful and varied floral designs is very fashionable now; they are printed, embroidered and woven. But all this flowering of seaside elegance will be half-covered by the beautiful summer gowns, cut like frock-coats, that are soft, terribly feminine, usually with large coloured lozenges on a blue ground, white piqué lapels and zip fasteners. The plain white ones have lapels and belts of floral or brightly-coloured material".

At the end of the decade, Dea presented rompers, that is to say one-piece sunsuits made up of a bodice and shorts gathered with elastic or ribbons at the thigh, and made of synthetic materials such as sniafiocco, costella and albene. Buttons, decorations and rings were made of galalite, a horn-like substance derived from casein, and were available in all colours.

86. Towards the mid-30's printed cotton, previously looked upon as a cheap material, began to be used for beachwear especially. *Le Jardin des Modes*, July 1936.

THE INGENIOUS FORTIES

MAKING A VIRTUE OF NECESSITY

Women's papers were devoting more and more space to gymnastics, illustrating and explaining various exercises for strengthening and improving the body. There was talk of "war holidays", of "difficult but glorious times for Our Country", the desperate energy-shortage and so forth, so that there was more delicacy in articles about beach-fashions: the rompers grew longer and more extravagant.

It was a time of ingenious clothing inventions that made up for the scarcity of materials.

Women were advised to make bathing-suits by using even "tiny bits of left-over material ... you only need a little fantasy and taste". The possibility of using old bits and pieces, usually considered as a tiresome nuisance filling up drawers, opened up numberless possibilities, and there were many practical examples, such as the strips of various materials used for the band of cloth worn as a brassiere, or

72

88.

patch-pockets as a form of decoration.

Documento Moda, the official publication of the National Fashion Institute, ran a competition in 1942 for finding new designs for material, probably in order to use creative ideas to compensate for the poor quality of the cloth turned out by the régime. Among the materials submitted, most of which were produced by famous 20th century Italian painters, there were some for "beach dresses and costumes, and pareos", including a "seaside subject" by

87. On the previous page: panorama of beach-fashion drawn by Brunetta Mateldi, who was to become one of the most celebrated fashion-illustrators of the last forty years of the 20th century. *Rakam*, May 1940.

88. Some variations are foreseen for summer 1940: bath-robes are shorter, shorts alternate with wide, brief skirts, the ancestors of the mini-skirt. Fantasy is represented by long "cellophane" skirts. *La Donna*, 1940.

89. Although by 1943 the war left little room for ideas of elegance, fashion-papers still showed some beach-wear, which might also be worn for leisure-times. *Fili Moda* n. 32, 1943.

89.

Carrà showing starfish, boats and splashes of pure colour, and "shells on the beach" by Filippo de Pisis.

Americans were wearing bathing-suits that were only to arrive in Europe ten years later. In this connection, I remember the amusing and colourful scene of a Disney film of the time (*The Three Caballeros*, 1943) in which Donald Duck flings himself into a beachful of bathing-beauties. Some were pretty young girls in bicoloured elasticized costumes moulded to the figure but completely covering the bottom, and others wore three-piece suits with brassiere, shorts and mini-skirt of bright self-colours or exotic floral motifs.

91.

The special nature of the material, which Europeans were to know as lastex, and its sheen, were visible from the effects of bright and opaque colours brought out by the Californian sun.

Some of the most celebrated bathing-suits were those worn by Esther Williams and her swimmers in their acquatic ballets, which delighted American cinemagoers as well as the spectators by the sides of the California and Florida swimming-pools.

90. Once the war was over in 1946, and although beaches had not yet been reorganized, beach-fashion began to design appropriate clothes again. *La Donna*, June 1946.

91. Esther Williams, the nautical ballerina who launched in the USA bathing-suits of velvet Lastex in her film "Neptune's daughter", 1949. Photo Farabola.

92.93. In 1949, Rochas, Schiaparelli and Pierre Balmain used towelling, printed cotton and woollen yersey for their beachwear. *Le Jardin des Modes*, July 1949.

90.

92.

THE DISTURBING BIKINI

While Italy was gaping awesomely at the buxom *Signorine Grandi Firme*, who seemed to burst out of their two-piece bathing-suits, made of a high band brasserie and swimming trunks, the Swiss designer Louis Reard and the famous couturier Jaques Heim were about to shock the world with their new creation. Presented in 1946, at the Piscine Molitar in Paris, when the first atom-bombs were tested on the Bikini atoll, this scanty bathing-suit, which completely unveiled stomach and navel, produced such an

93.

EMO

Maillots de bain

94. The bikini becomes part of swimsuit-makers' repertoire. Emo, *maillot de bain. Le Jardin des Modes, Juin* 1949.

95.

explosive effect that its creators decided to change its name from *Atome* to *Bikini*.

The bikini challenge, however, was not taken up until the end of the 40's. In 1949, *Elle* presented three daring models that were ahead of the period as regards the amount of leg shown.

But few were the daring women who wore them, so much so that the bikini-pioneers' names are still remembered. They were Micheline Bernardin, a Franch ballet-dancer, and Adriana Benetti, an Italian actress.

In Italy and Spain the sanctimonious morality of the time, closely watched by long-established clericalism, made women prefer revivals, and accept the return of myriad-striped combinations, thereby demonstrating the rule of physics that every action has its equal and opposite reaction. In the more emancipated but equally puritan United States the bikini was worn only in private until the beginning of the 60', when it made its appearence on public beaches and swimming-pools.

Originality and elegance were typical of those years, even if creativity was sometimes rather vulgar, seeming to try to obliterate the suffering and anguish of the war.

The first "fishermen's" trousers began to appear; there were also clinging trousers, worn with an overskirt open in front, or with fringed tunics. Korean straw hats and sombreros flourished, or wide crownless brims over hair gathered in low buns or hidden beneath scarves.

There was also a return to woollen costumes with the inevitable figure of the swimming girl embroidered on the mini-skirt; scarves and sashes were knotted at the waist. Materials were striped, polka-dotted; there were childish checks, festooned hemlines, trimmings, ribbons and *broderie anglaise*.

95. A drawing by Sormani illustrates costumes for swimming, sunbathing and lying on the beach. Summer 1946. *La Donna*, June 1946.

96. Looms and spinning-mills prepare specialized cloths for bathing-suits. *Le Jardin des Modes,* July 1949.

97. Lucia Bosè, star of the 1950's Italian cinema, wears a tiny bikini on the Venice Lido for the Cinema Festival. *La Settimana Incom,* 9 September 1950.

UPROAR AND KITSCH: THE FIFTIES

AN OUTRAGE TO DECENCY: A FEW CENTIMETRES TOO ... LITTLE

Nor was it in the 50's that the bikini, although accepted and nonchalantly worn by stars and would-be stars (Silvana Pampanini, Gina Lollobrigida, Silva Koscina, Rossana Podestà and Marisa Allasio among the Italians, and Brigitte Bardot in France) succeeded in becoming a fashion-phenomenon, in Italy at least.

In reality, it was always considered scandalous by the majority, and caused an uproar if worn on public beaches; wearers ran the risk of ending up in gaol for offending what was known as "an ordinary sense of decency".

This measure was decreed by Onorevole Scelba Sudati, then Minister of the Interior. Policemen patrolled the beaches, a tailor's tape-measure in hand, in search of pretty girls wearing two-pieces or young bloods in slips, to see whether the garments were in order. In Spain, no measurements were necessary: the bikini was quite simply forbidden.

At the time, sex was scandalous for the mere fact of existing, and even the strip-tease numbers allowed at the time ended with the girl wearing a tiny bikini. Nor was it only the Italian Minister who ostracized the two-piece; there was a great to-do in England because of a photograph of Princess Margaret wearing such a costume when leaving the yacht of a magnate (perhaps the Aga Khan) and snapped with a telephoto lens by a "candid cameraman" on holiday at what was not yet the Costa Smeralda.

98.

Current prudery in Europe forbade the wearing of bikinis in public places. In reality, all the ladies belonging to the nomadic society that frequents the high places of international fame all the year round, were caught in "mini" costumes by the usual scoop-seeking photographers, turning their telephotos onto private swimming-pools. The pictures the illustrated weeklies (the Italians are famous for this kind of literature)

transmitted to their readers were nearly always out of focus and blurred, showing that whoever took the photo was either up in a tree, behind a bush or balancing on the window-ledge of a building opposite.

Popular reviews for women still showed prim little tunics with flared mini-skirts, double-breasted bodices, short socks, short-sleeved shirts and floating skirts.

98.99. The sunsuit-idea extends to dresses, or to the combination of swimsuit and skirt that transforms beachwear into an elegant morning dress.
Donne eleganti, Summer 1951.

LASTEX TRIUMPHS
AND TOWELLING IS BACK

The one piece satin Lastex costume with a mini-skirt over the groin remains the dominant style.

The papers report: "the free and easy beach-fashions include no real novelties; what is new are the pratical cotton jackets, and towelling, which had been abandoned".

Sorelle Fontana's combined jacket and bath-robe is in blue towelling, cloth lined with white and red stripes, like the brassiere and slip, and is reversible. There is talk of a "sunsuit" with motifs of "little knotted aprons" or of little printed cotton handkerchiefs.

Bright colours are to the fore "as well as classic white and the usual black, orange, coral-red, yellow and green are to be seen".

"Very exposed two-pieces (i.e. with the navel showing) are only worn on boats, while for the beach it is always fashionable to wear a costume with an open jacket, or, better still, the straight or pleated little tunic".

On the balconies of beach-huts, where the sun is filtered through the matting

100.

above, girls plaster themselves with cream, or comb their short wet hair, wearing little suits with "American" collars (very high on the neck and "excavated" over the shoulders to expose the shoulder-blades), large straw hats held to the back by laces that fall onto the chest, and necklaces of murexes or pebbles.

The slip may be fastened at the hips with a series of parallel cords, through which peeps out the bronzed skin beneath.

On Capri, one walks about in very short trousers clinging to the stomach, known as shorts, and shirts made out of handkerchiefs knotted at shoulder-level, or in "fishermen's" parti-coloured trousers, held at the waist with drapes and scarves, or tunics with turned - over new necklines.

The classic beach get-up consists of "four pieces": printed cloth bodice and mini-skirt, a real skirt, and a tiny bolero,"enabling the bather to move, without too much changing, from the cool water of the pool to the torrid city streets".

100.101. Fath uses cotton-jersey for his striped, 1920-ish costume, while for sunbathing he neverthless recommends a bikini. Printed cotton Dior's *ensemble*, and another model by Jacques Fath, who suggests a red cloth tunic with matching, towelling-lined jacket. Photo Interstampa. *La Donna,* June 1950.

101.

84

102.

[signature: Pezzi]

DRAPERY, WHALEBONE
AND SEQUINS

In 1952, fringes were added to light, wide-brimmed coloured straw hats. Sandals were much in evidence with thin leather lacing round the ankle.

There are advertisements for costumes "made of material gathered on the inside with elastic threads", creating drapery.

Carven launched a "one-piece costume-vest, with a short clinging underskirt", *trompe l'oeil* motifs like belts, sashes and shaded colouring to give the illusion of a smaller waistline. The

neckline is often heart-shaped - also the fashion for evening-dresses - and shoulder-straps are optional.

Cole of California, a famous Italian manufacturer of American-licence bathing-costumes, advertised Lastex suits printed in a wide variety of designs.

During the 50's the concept of sexiness was always linked with provocation, curves, aggressive breasts; when the hips were not exuberant enough they were emphasized with drapery and frills.

Wrapping, padded and reinforced by whalebones in the crucial points were also the costumes worn by the girls at the Miss Italia contests, among which the actresses Gina Lollobrigida and Sophia Loren.

Made in shiny satin-lastex, with silk and sequin embroideries, and far more

102. An *Armonia* bathing-suit of elasticized cloth, designed by Maria Pezzi. *Bellezza,* May 1953.

103. Bikini and wrap of printed silk are a classic of sea-side elegance. Photo Gianni Della Valle.

103.

104.

suitable for starring in a revue than for a beach or a swimming-pool, bathing-costumes were very much inspired to the phony Olympic style sported by Esther Williams and her aquatic dancers in the movies, and were worn whenever a minimum of glamour was required.

These swimsuits, branded as too tacky in the *nudelook* period, can be regarded as the bad copy of more famous ones, worn by Hollywood stars and American ladies both in private and in films. These costumes were beautiful, flattering and saught-after and were produced by a well-known American firm that was entering the élite European market right at the beginning of the 50's, when war and reconstruction were over and Europe was yearning for novelty and luxury.

Tipically, Catalina started as a *lingerie* firm in 1907 and, thanks to John Benz, soon began to produce jersey bathing-suits. During the 30's Catalina replaced jersey with Lastex, the elastic fibre that adheres to the line of the body and comes in bright colours, finally emphasizing waistline and breasts.

104. Following the fashion of those years, the one-piece elastic bathing-suit enhances and emphasizes the waistline, *Mani di Fata*, 50's.

105.

106.

THE DEFEAT OF THE PIN-UPS

Novità, the Italian review for elegant women, declared in June 1955: "Bathing- and beach-suits are back to one-piece, in Lastex or simple cotton cloth, to the detriment of two- or three-piece costumes, bikinis or any other exposed formula that predominated during the past few years, on the pretext and in favour of sunbathing". It went on: "Some new costumes come up to the shoulders, leaving exposed only the large round neckline. The colours, when not abdicating in favour of black, are light: strawberry-pink and lemon-yellow seem to be the favourites".

Make-up should be lighter: "eyes are not outlined almond-shape in black (the gazelle-eyes of last year- rather theatrical) but shaded in grey or green".

Short and simple hair-dos "need the touch of a little trimming; a ribbon tied by the milliner, a rose or bunch of jasmin, a wing worn as a crown, anything showing a certain amount of care".

"Young lady" style is fashionable for women of all ages: "graceful, chaste women have beaten the bewitching pin-ups ".

107.

In 1956, loops for ribbons, knots and bows emphasize the neckline and the waist, which has decended to the hips. A costume of sateen and flowered poplin, or one with a heart-shaped neckline and a short, three-flounced clinging skirt, are pronounced classics.

Vertical stripes which "make you look svelte and thinner", are suggested for the piqué tunic-jacket, to be worn over short trousers.

105. Marilyn Monroe, America's sweetheart, in the film *Niagara* (1953). She wears a chaste bikini on Malibu beach. Photo Farabola, Milan.

106. Marilyn Monroe during the shooting of *As Young as You Are*. She is wearing a classic Lastex suit without shoulder-straps. Photo Farabola, Milan.

107. A good bathing-suit can emphasize the charms of beauty-queens. Eight international beauties at a fashion show in Munich. *Tempo,* 27 March 1958.

108. During a moment of glamour at the Venice Film Festival of 1955, English actress Diana Dors wears a mink bikini. P. Silmon, *The Bikini.*

108.

109.

110.

ITALIAN SIMPLICITY

Maria Pezzi, a leading fashion-journalist, writes in *Il Giorno* about the Italian Style that is all the rage abroad. It is easily defined: "the whole secret lies in being simple without going too far in that direction. For ten years now, at Capri and Portofino, women have been wearing more or less the same trousers, the same masculine-type shirts and the same cloth sunsuits. Only Swiss women appear on our beaches wearing ballet-dancers' *tutus*, hoping to look romantic. Everything depends on details, on colours and the juxtaposition of these unchanging garments".

Sunsuits can also be hand-painted in wide brush-strokes, and held up with a single strap rising like a collar from the centre of the bust.

Shorts to the knee, Bermuda-style, a little overall, a jacket with a wide collar that can turn into a hood and a *foulard* over the short knotted like a pareo at the waist are the beach-fashion novelties for 1957.

109.110. At the end of the 50's, Mediterranean islands become holiday resorts: Capri, Ischia and Ponza were popular, while Ibiza, Panarea and Corfu remained reserved to the élite, and inspired beach-fashion. *Annabella* n. 32, 11 August 1957.

111. For beach-games and protection against the wind, cotton shirts with coloured stripes, alternately smooth and goffered, are imported from America.
Novità, February 1958.

112. Between the '50s and '60s Parah adds its first helanca bathing-suits to the *Lingerie* collections.

111.

112.

114.

90

113.

Accessories include a towelling turban
to hide wet hair after bathing, bathing-
caps with rubber rose petals, just arrived
from America, with matching bags, a
foulard to wrap round the head and then
knot behind the nape, sandals made of
straw, towelling or coloured leather with
shoelaces of the same material and the
sunsuit, a "striped three-piece" consisting
of a hair-ribbon, ballet-slippers with elastic
loops and a little bag to hang over the big
straw one.

Nor should one definitely renounce the
tent-robe: "loose, wide and soft, it's an
ideal thing for the beach. It chimes in with

the flou look and so is up-to-date and pratical". Wrapped in it, you can change quickly without too many people looking.

Every day more emphasis is placed on "class"; the best way of appreciating the quality of a lady is to see whether she behaves on the beach with the same natural spontaneity as when she is fully dressed. For this reason, those who cannot wear a bikini as though it were a *princesse* or an ordinary sports get-up are counselled to desist.

113.-116. For up-to-dateness on the beach, here are swim-and-sun-suits in knitted cotton or silk, completed by fashionable accessories: hats, tunics and handbags. *Vogue France*, 1959.

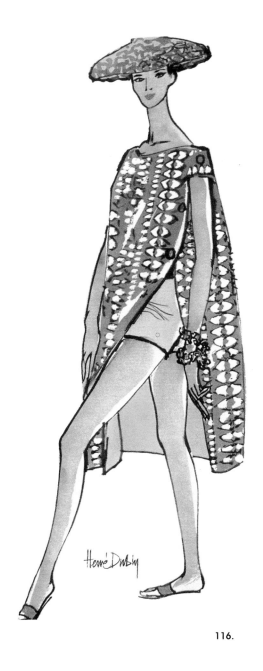

116.

At the end of the 50's, the accent was still placed on well-known styles, with an attempt to fit them to the physique of the wearer; shorts for those with good legs, towelling for the skinny, a low neckline for the short woman and the tunic with a long slenderizing waistline for those overweight.

There were short-and-shirt get-ups (long sleeves, turned-down collars, patch pockets and slits on the hips) with the shorts only a little longer than the shirt. They were made up in printed silk with crowded motifs along the row of buttons like 18th century waistcoats.

115.

117. Seaside holidays also imply elegant originality. A bathing-costume cut like a high-fashion dress. *L'Officiel,* 1959.

TWENTY YEARS OF
TURBULENT FASHION

BEACHES FOR ALL
AND FOR ALL TASTES

The 60's, later to be called fabulous, began very quietly, though they ended in the revolutionary hubbub of juvenile contestation.

The Venice Lido had by then acquired at least five beaches, to suit every taste and social category.

From the Hotel Des Bains to be Excelsior, the grand-hotel zone offered its select, refined international clientele, when arriving in August and September, cabins provided with every comfort and perfect service; all was clean and silent, though busier during the afternoon *thé dansant*. One ate in the elegant restaurants, or just nibbled something light so as not to blow out the stomach.

The public beach, on the other hand, divided into sectors A B & C, with more sand than the Grand Hotels, did not provide hot water in the showers. It was frequented by middle and lower-middle class Venetians, and animated by games of volley-ball, tambourine-ball, and marbles and sand-castles for the children. In its two restaurants, the first juke-boxes

118. Design by Chino Bert for a J. Esterel model. *Arianna,* July 1960.

shrilled happily away, surrounded by muscular, handsome "beach-boys" bent on innocent flirtation.

Normal-sized meals were eaten in the cabins, as if at home, followed by beach teas.

It was customary for the boys to come to the beach in the morning, followed by the womenfolk arriving towards one o'clock with hot food. There was no attempt at roughing it, and the drinks were kept cool by being buried in the wet sand, wrapped up in wet cloths.

After a long stretch of beach belonging to the hospital and used by patients and nurses, one came to the public beach at S.

Nicoletto, noisy, colourful and frequented by the poorer classes. Here the meals were "blow-outs", almost a hymn to the joy of living. Field-kitchens were organized, and, in defiance of etiquette and good manners, feasting went on joyously. They sang, joked, listened to the radio and danced, just as at home.

Further along still was an area where among spiky dunes and cement bunkers left over from the war, it was not advisable to go, because, as the mothers would whisper, it was full of sex-fiends, peeping Toms and homosexuals.

In all these places costumes were the same; elasticized and chaste, still with the

94

119.

119. A towelling "baby-doll" can also serve as a beach-suit for expectant mothers. Drawing by Fiora Gandolfi. *Lo Specchio,* 28 May 1961.

120.121. During the early 60's, one-piece costumes are still the favourite: in cotton or Lycra: a new synthetic material, very light, elastic and printable. Two-pieces are beautified by fringes and flounces. Drawing by Fiora Gandolfi. *Lo Specchio,* 21 May, 4 June 1961.

121.

122.

mini-skirt over the groin; little beach *ensembles* worthy of an 18th century revival. Very new and fantastic, though, were the bathing-caps, with petals, overlapping scales or ruffles.

The "minimum suitcase" suggested for a week-end by the sea was little different from that thought requisite for a month's stay at the beginning of the century. "Apart from a change of linen and a nightdress, you need an overall, a matching shirt and shorts, a shirt to match long trousers, several *foulards*, a scarf, a low-necked dress, two necklaces and a jet-covered evening-bag. Then in the bag, you will need, beside the bath-robe or the optional bath-sheet, two bathing-suits, a bathing-cap, a sweater, a nylon shirt for motorboating, two pairs of ballet-slippers, a pair of sandals for the beach and another for the evening, and finally bedroom slippers, flippers and a mask". Flippers and mask were there just to chime in with Edoardo Vianello, who sang the famous hit played by every *juke-boxe* in the '60s: "Abbronzatissima sotto i raggi del sole", and to dive into the blue sea with spear gun and underwater goggles.

122. Specialized swimwear manufacturers advertize their models in fashion-papers. These, by Cole of California, in Rodiatoce nylon, form part of 1963's rich collection. *Grazia,* 30 June 1963.

123. Fashion-papers of the 60's frequently refer to the elegance of the one-piece costume.
Photo Gianni Della Valle.

124. *Triumph* bathing-suits are studied in every detail to highlight the wearer's figure. The brassiere is sometimes incorporated. *Grazia,* 3 May 1964.

123.

THE SAINT TROPEZ STYLE

At St Tropez, the ultra-*chic* beach where the Vips from all over the world met every season, in the apparently static and frigid climate of the 60's, Brigitte Bardot launched costumes and bikinis in baby patterns and materials - checks and little hearts *broderie anglaise* and lace ribbons tied in knots on the hips, always threatening to get undone. In Italy the actress Marisa Allasio contributed to the diffusion of this style, that was flattering for young and buxom girls, but tended to emphasize wrinkles and make elder women look extremely ridicolous.

It was a time of bizarre hairdressing, with much false hair, wigs - some of them made of plastic - plastic jewellery, artificial flowers showily displayed on matching swimsuits. Make-up gave all women bigger

124.

125.

and lovelier eyes, with shadow on the lids, and eyelashes either false or pencilled in under the eyes.

It was also a time of great changes in art, painting and sculpture, and the Op and Pop movements had their effects on materials, clothes and taste. The Hippies, Mary Quant, Pierre Cardin, Courrèges and rock music influenced mentalities and behaviour.

Novelties came thick and fast: Saint Tropez bodices fastened under the bosom, worn with Tahitian bermudas that left the belly naked up to the navel, bikinis with padded brassieres and triangle-cut slips resting low on the hips, with a shortening effect for the thigh, metal and plastic decorations, lace and beads and crochet-work.

126.

125. A scanty two-piece bathing-suit in colours fashionable in the 60's. Photo Gianni Della Valle.

126. Two-piece and pareo for the Ken Scott bathing-suit. *Grazia*, 1967.

127.

127.128. Printed towelling bikini (1967) and velvet-towelling barracan with matching bathing-suit.
All in the classical bright and vivid colours typical of Emilio Pucci's collections. Photo Lumachi, Florence.

TITLED COSTUMES

The Fontana Sisters launched the cabin-costume: a huge Ku Klux Klan cowl which covered the legs to mid-thigh and had only two slits for the eyes. But during the '60s, the leading role in the history of bathing-suits and accessories was undoubtedly played by Marquis Emilio Pucci, depicted in 1963 by fashion journalist Eugenia Sheppard - maybe with a bit too much emphasis - as *the richest and most famous designer in the world*. As a matter of fact, the printed silk bikinis designed by this incredible *Arbiter Elegantiae*, whose taste was to bewitch women of every age and nationality over the decades, were a must in the wardrobe of the jet-set, especially in the United States. Together with the bikinis, Emilio Pucci's beach get-ups included bags, blouses, silk organzine overalls printed with colourful motifs of various inspiration: from Mexican folk designs to optical patterns, from the reproduction of the Monreale mosaics to the stained-glass windows of cathedrals and the colours of the Palio di Siena quarters. Trousers were in stretch shantung, with matching blouses in the brightest colours conceivable at the

128.

time: apple green, saffron yellow, and turquoise.

And while the orientalizing and folk styles, launched by Lancetti, brought to the beaches costumes that covered one ambiguously, turbans or *kefiyeh* variously wound round the head, making bathers look like odalisques, Tahitians or gypsies, Mila Schön showed bathing-suits for the evening, of white tulle covered all over with strass, little beads and *sequins*, the slip and top assymetrical.

SYNTHETIC FIBRES

The great majority of Italian-made bathing-suits, with the exception of the famous and successful creations by Emilio Pucci, were manufactured by small, experienced *lingerie* firms that subsequently specialized in beachwear and gave origin to today's top-quality labels.

In fact, throughout the whole decade, women who could not find the right style or size among the ready-to-wear costumes would have beautiful one- or two-pieces made to measure by their own corset-makers. This custom was so widespread that in the United States the standard jersey or lastex one-piece, sewn with elastic thread, typical of the '40s, was called *dressmaker swimsuit*.

Meanwhile, a new elastic fibre, extremely light and thinner than a human hair, had conquered the market and opened up a whole wide range of possibilities to the new-born industry: it was called Lycra (trademark registered in the whole world by Du Pont), and its

129. Beachwear designed by Walter Albini for *Cole of*

130.

132.

131.

introduction signed the end of helanaca bathing-suits (a very elastic synthetic fibre often used for stockings, that after bathing absorbed water and took a long time to dry), and the irreversible downfall of Lastex.

By the end of the 60's, the elastomer created in 1959 in the United States by the French researcher Eleuthère Irenée Du Pont de Nemours as a substitute of rubber for the *lingerie* industry, had attained a major role in the swmisuit industry. "Lycra brought about a real revolution in beachwear, and made it possible to create bathing-suits of extraordinary qualitiy: it is very light, adheres graciously to the body following its contours, dries quickly, is very resistent to perspiration and swimming-pool chlorine, and comes in a

130.131. The Lycra costumes by *Armonia* are to the fore in the '60s: this has a sort of "shell" neckline held up by a cord round the neck. Armonia marchio Lycra. Photo Gianni Della Valle.

132. Beach-eccentricity for the 60's includes an improbable costume with sleeves for conferring a lozenge-shaped tan. Photo Gianni Della Valle.

wide variety of prints and very bright colours", stated Giampiero Boschetti, marketing manager at Du Pont Italy, thirty years later.

The assets of the new material were not appreciated immediately by all: it was dismissed by many as too daring, as it hid nothing of the female body; but nonetheless, the firms that introduced Lycra were offered extraordinary opportunities to produce sample collections that in a short time became complete lines, and served as a point of reference for designers that at the time were beginning to launch their labels.

In their Summer issues, women's weekly magazines like *Grazia*, *Arianna*, *Amica* presented the collections by Armonia, a firm that had entered the market in the '50s, and in the mid-sixties, thanks to an accurate choice and succesful combination of materials, designs, colours and styles, became an appreciated leader in its field.

133.

134.

AN EMERGING PHENOMENON

After the cultural revolution of 1968, when feminists publicly burned bras, garter belts and any other example of constrictive underwear considered a male imposition, Parah, the *lingerie* firm created at the beginnng of the 50's by the curset-maker Edda Paracchini Piazzalunga, began to diversify its production and launched its first line of helanca bathing-suits.

133. Sporting swimmers prefer one-piece costumes. Photo Gianni Della Valle.

134. By the mid-60's, the bikini brassiere becomes a bodice, known as St. Tropez, from the resort where it was launched. Photo Gianni Della Valle.

135. A spectacular muslin cape covers the tiny bikini. Model by Fausto Sarli, Naples. Photo Gianni Della Valle.

136. Some metres of material cut on the cross and cleverly draped take the place of a sun-suit. An idea from Giorgio Benussi Trani.

136.

135.

Thanks to its scientific knowledge of the female anatomy and to its long experience in underwear and *lingerie*, in 1970 Parah converted most of its production to beachwear: bathing-suits, bathrobes and sunsuits. The collections were a result of the firm's thorough understanding of the consumer's demands. At first using helanca and then Lycra for bathing-suits, as well as polyamide for accessories, Parah managed to respect the natural needs of a breathing body without cutting down on originality and elegance.

The first collections of one-piece costumes and bikinis already anticipated the future trend that Parah contributed to launch: the introduction of bathing-suits in fashion collections, and the establishment of the "fashion bathing-costume" as an independent phenomenon.

104

137.

138.

140.

137.-141. Examples of 60's beachwear. Summer holidays are spent at fashionable resorts - the Italian Riviera, the Côte d'Azur, and all Meditteranean islands, with a preference for Sardinia. Photo Gianni Della Valle.

This get-up, promptly named "topless", was designed in England by Belleville Sassoon and produced in Hollywood.

The impact of the 'licentious' bathing-suit on Italian beaches triggered off different and polemical reactions, often caused by the beautiful foreign girls (Germans, Scandinavians or Americans) on vacation, whose confidence with their

142. In 1966, Ken Scott used the same printed pattern for a Lycra one-piece, a cotton two-piece, and silk organdi turban and cape draped round the head.
La Donna, 1966.

143. The beach-set is the all the rage. Top and flares (100% polyamide) with coordinated bathing-suit (helanca and Brill Nylon) make up a winning triplet.
Parah catalogue, 1971-1972.

142.

BREASTS AND MORALITY: THE END OF CENSORSHIP

In the summer of 1970, six years after its first appeerence in the United States - where it struck like a thunderbolt from the blue to shock the world with its provocative challenge - the topless style landed in Europe, on the trendy and ultra-*chic* beach of Saint Tropez.

On 20 June 1964, an American model named Tom Lee Shelley appeared in public on the shores of Lake Michigan with a high (but blonde) Nefertiti hair-do: her bathing-suit consisted of clinging shorts, cut high enough to cover the navel, held up by braces crossed over the bare chest.

143.

144. Ready to tune in with the trend of the moment, in 1977 Parah launched an advertisement campaign with giant billboards (6 x 3 m) showing model Barbara d'Urso winkinig from the back and wearing only the slip of a Parah bikini. An epoch-making image.

145.

146.

bodies was still unknown to the Italians. The latter, though on their way to emancipation, had not yet broken loose from the last moral restraints. But after having overcome the initial imbarassment, it was just a question of finding the right time and place to expose bare breasts that at least had to be... presentable. Common sense and good manners prevailed, as well as caution, because malice and censorship always lied in wait.

When faced with bare breasts, magistrates reacted differently, according to their mentality.

For example, in 1977, magistrate Giaccardi acquitted two girls from Leghorn caught wearing monokinis on the beach at Voltri, justifying his decision in these terms: "the simple exposure of the naked female breast, unaccompanied by lascivious exhibitions (soliciting), can by no means be considered as offensive to the ordinary sense of decency, as it is an action completely foreign to manifestations of a sexual nature, and not intended to excite concupiscence".

However, "notwithstanding the fact that it was now clear that Italian customs, though traditionally slow and reluctant to comply with standards accepted in other countries for some time, had acquired a mentality that could not be scandalized or feel unease or emotion at the sight of a women's breasts" (G. Salimbeni), an intransigent magistrate of Palermo called Salmeri had the courage to reply: "It is ingenuous to think, bearing in mind the impulses of Nature, that the sole intention of these dauntless women and girls who so boldly show off (while caring not at all for

145. Low-necked dress, one-piece costume and scanty two-piece (in polyamide and elastam) are the three practical elements for the new set. *Parah* catalogue, Summer 1977. Foto Bottino.

146. *Armonia'* s Lycra model *Brigitte*, from the 1979 collection. *Vogue*, May 1979.

147. Fresh from the USA, the monokini appears on European beaches. In France, during the early 70's, it was reserved for young bodies on exclusive beaches. *Marie Claire*, May 1978.

148. *Armonia* used printed jerseylon with a coloured firework-pattern for the one-piece costume and the long dress, of clearly Indian inspiration, in line with the ethnic trend of the early 70's.

the special sensibilities of the children present) intimate portions of their bodies, is to benefit completely from the sun's rays. There is an erotic thrill in the pleasure derived from the unbridled freedom of exposure and the mischeivous knowledge that one's body, freed from the protection of clothing, is caressed by the inevitably concupiscent stares of men blessed with normal sexuality".

In 1979, taking inspiration from the trend of the moment, Parah launched a campaign that was to become legendary: a model that waved in the air the useless top part of her bikini.

148.

147.

149.

150.

FROM ONE SCANDAL...
TO THE OTHER

Meanwhile the tanga arrived from South America.

Legless and worn high over the hips, it was not suited to everyone: if it was justifiable on a savage, with feathers in the hair and rings in the nose, it became complete nonsense on the beach. Better stay naked or wear a towel round the waist and go topless: the effect was more natural and less vulgar. The tanga also required a more extensive depilation, reducing the pubic triangle of protohistorical memory to a ridicolous narrow taft. The undisputed success of this style, that was applied also to the back part of one-piece costumes, was undoubtedly promoted by permissive ideas and sexual emancipation, and cuold be an interesting subject for psycoanalytical and anthropological researches.

By the end of the 70's the one-piece costume had returned, hailed as an "original revival" and a "masterpiece of fashion". Readers were told that, for swimming and sunbathing, "a touch of high fashion gives the whole costume a more dressy appearance, thanks to the use of ruching and draping".

Special costumes for pregnant women also appeared in Italy; they had now acquired the right to expose their swollen bodies to the beneficial effects of sea and sun without false shame.

149. Tanga. Yes or no? Photo Hans Feurer. *Vogue*, May 1977.

150. The isle of Timor, famous for its paradise-birds living in the woods, gave its name to this bikini from 1978 Parah's collection.

Many two-piece and bikini models that matched the bra with boxer-shorts or bermuda trousers were designed to be sold as a set with one-piece costumes.

There were many types of fashionable neckline; tops without shoulder-straps, either held in place by a straight band or by metal slides at the sides and in the middle. Deep necklines were in evidence, some of them descending as far as the waist.

Decoration took the form of cords, beads and slender chains. All collections showed solar and tropical themes, some of them interesting imitations of the skins of leopards, snakes and other animals.

151. Towards the end of the 60's bathing-costumes were worn without false shame even by pregnant women.

152. A tiny *cache-sexe* mitigates a drastic nudity, with a sleeved sun-top, short to the waist and with a wide neckline leaving the shoulders bare. *Mare Marvel. Vogue,* May 1977.

151.

152.

153. One-piece costumes need an original touch. A snake outlines the neckline of this model from *La Perla Mare*, reminiscent of Tarzan's adventures or, given its position, Eve's temptation in a modern key. *Vogue*, May 1979.

A POLLUTED TURN
OF THE CENTURY

154. Ever since the early '80s, Italian beachwear fashion trends were launched and defined by specialized manufacturers. Parah, 1983 collection.

TWO DECADES OF POLLUTION
THE CULT OF APPEARANCES

After the fabuolus 60's, and the dramatic '70s (that in Italy were named 'leaden years') came the unrestrained 80's, also defined as 's... years' (just to quote Monsieur Cambronne), by the Italian ideologist Roberto d'Agosino who is an expert in narcissism, individualism and hedonism.

The cathegorical imperative of the 80's was "appearance"; people had to build themselves a 'look', an external image, so as to keep up with their professional, political or mundane role, (sometimes real and sometimes only ideal).

The body was still to the foreground and its cult in progressive and ostentatious expansion. To make it the attractive reflection of a serene, satisfied and optimistic Ego, body-building, dancing, squash, water-massage and Jacuzzis became necessary, and the garments worn in these occasions had the same style, dimensions and functionality of bathing-suits.

The philosophy of appearance, promoted by the media and fashion designers, became widespread among all social classes: quality was now identified with designer clothes, and the 80's are full of labels: celebrated, famous, actual, modern ones, on every garment or accessory.

155.156. By the 80's, beachwear had become an important chapter in the economics of fashion. Entire collections, which dealt with every aspect in the smallest detail, were produced. Gucci. *Elle* 1981.

114

155.

156.

The bathing-costume, that was to undergo many transformations by designers, faced the 80's with the always actual and never solved dilemma - one- or two-piece?

Such a problem would have been unthinkable only two or three years earlier, when subscription to a more or less complete nudism had seized most women; but now the one-piece was back and livlier than ever. Thanks to the specialized manufacturers, the new one-piece costume was perfectly shaped, with extremely clear-cut and definite lines, and had finally turned into a real garment.

A new and special niche in the beachwear market of the early 80's was represented by women from the American province and by "on the road" travellers,

157.

158.

159.

who needed extremely versatile and comfortable clothes: functional garments easily transformable into more sober ones for formal occasions. Americans demanded a wardrobe made up of few pieces that could be adapted to the different situations with few touches, and were meant to be squeezed into the backpack together with a myriad of other objects necessary to travelling, The right answer came from La Perla, an Italian *lingerie* manufacturer that entered the beachwear market in the 60's: the new creation was a Lycra costume softly draped and easily transformable into a sheath dress with a rapid movement.

Although the bikini remained an all-time favourite, the "magic moment" experienced by one-piece costumes was equally undeniable, and the new legless and strapless styles that enabled an extensive suntan were the proof that it was not a mere rediscovery or revival. "The new one-piece is quite different, thanks to

157. A fanciful interpretation of Lycra beach-dress, ensuring ease of movement and a well-dressed look. *MB International* Collection, 1982.

158. Strapless Lycra one piece bathing-suit with insertions of different colours. *Swan original. Vogue*, May 1982.

159. A well-structured beachwear collection guarantees exquisite elegance from morning till night. *Parah Collection*, 1986.

160.

scale: the majority served to testify the designers' effort in beachwear collections produced on licence. The beachwear of the "big numbers", the sought-after bathing-suits, the same that flattered the figure and filled the trendy beaches at every new season, remained the exclusive prerogative of leading beachwear manufacturers, like La Perla and Parah.

160. Giorgio Armani for *Yacktex. Vogue*, early '80s.

161. The one-piece costume is revised: this is low-necked and decidedly legless. Sabbia, 1985.

162. Lycra and polyamide bathing-suit. The waistline is enhanced by a sash closed with a sequin flower on the hip. Oleg Cassini. Photo Bob Krieger.

163. One-piece costume of assymetrical cut in white Lycra with colourful prints. Christian Dior, 1984.

164. Essential and exquisitely dressy the two-piece by Ferré Beachware. Photo Herb Ritts, 1988.

the efforts of designers, who within a few years have transformed it into an element of decisive importance in building the fashion-image of women in the summer" (Di Forti).

As a matter of fact, the designer bathing-costume was something made for the catwalk, a necessary part of the ready-to-wear system created by the very designers: it was there to prove the authority of a label that controlled and set the standards for a complete collection.

And though there is no denying the quality and fantasy that characterized designer bathing-suits, only very few of them were actually produced on a large

162.

163.

THE FANTASY OF DESIGNERS

1986 signed the 40th birthday of the bikini, that despite a small drop of popularity still maintained its role on the beaches: strapless brasserie and legless slip resting high over the hips were worn with shirts, blouses and so on. The Olympic style, too, had been revived; one-piece, elastic, a second skin, with a deeper, harmonious neckline to emphasize the shoulders and cancel any suspicion of masculinity.

The solutions proposed by designers were an attractive combination of elegance, seduction and fun. The variations on the theme were almost infinite, from Fendi's ultra-legless one-pieces, that at the end of the decade will be inspired to the motifs of the trans-avant-garde art movements, to Krizia's Olympic costumes, worn with long black shiny gloves, that the designer herself defined as multi-functional garments.

According to Moschino one- or two-piece costumes had become status Symbols, and he played about with the arsenal of lace and ribbons proper to *lingerie*, and launched one-pieces with writings on, with which the wearer was supposed to identify.

164.

165. A zipped costume sums up the aggressive tendencies of 80's fashion. Sabbia, *Linea Intima,* 1987.

166.167. Models by Versace, Moschino, Schön and Coveri. Drawing by Michele Futsch for *Fashion,* 12 September 1988.

165.

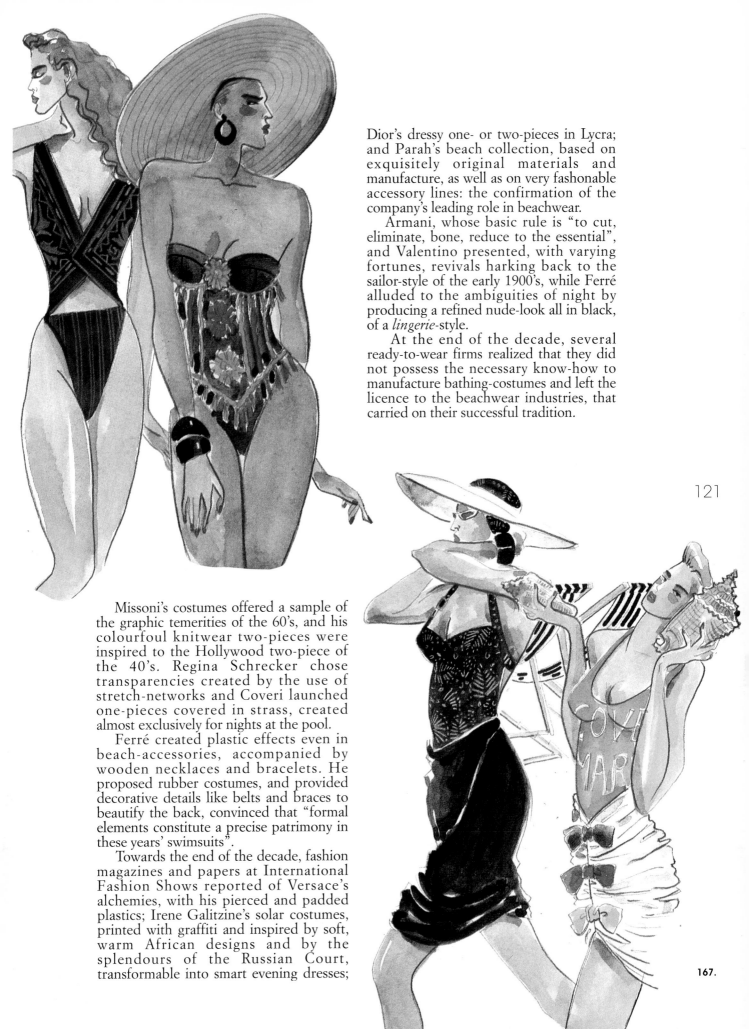

Dior's dressy one- or two-pieces in Lycra; and Parah's beach collection, based on exquisitely original materials and manufacture, as well as on very fashonable accessory lines: the confirmation of the company's leading role in beachwear.

Armani, whose basic rule is "to cut, eliminate, bone, reduce to the essential", and Valentino presented, with varying fortunes, revivals harking back to the sailor-style of the early 1900's, while Ferré alluded to the ambiguities of night by producing a refined nude-look all in black, of a *lingerie*-style.

At the end of the decade, several ready-to-wear firms realized that they did not possess the necessary know-how to manufacture bathing-costumes and left the licence to the beachwear industries, that carried on their successful tradition.

121

Missoni's costumes offered a sample of the graphic temerities of the 60's, and his colourfoul knitwear two-pieces were inspired to the Hollywood two-piece of the 40's. Regina Schrecker chose transparencies created by the use of stretch-networks and Coveri launched one-pieces covered in strass, created almost exclusively for nights at the pool.

Ferré created plastic effects even in beach-accessories, accompanied by wooden necklaces and bracelets. He proposed rubber costumes, and provided decorative details like belts and braces to beautify the back, convinced that "formal elements constitute a precise patrimony in these years' swimsuits".

Towards the end of the decade, fashion magazines and papers at International Fashion Shows reported of Versace's alchemies, with his pierced and padded plastics; Irene Galitzine's solar costumes, printed with graffiti and inspired by soft, warm African designs and by the splendours of the Russian Court, transformable into smart evening dresses;

167.

168.

169.

DIFFERENT INTERPRETATIONS

Beach fashions for the end of the 80's are of all sorts, with wahlebones and belts, romantic or space-age, with somptuous drapery or full of laces, strings and little cords.

The materials used are futuristic, and seem to glow with their own light: metallized, laminated, perforated, zipped up, rubberized, quilted, patterned, - all meant to define the body's structure and to show that after one single century, or a little more, much still remains to be invented in the history of the bathing-costume.

Certainly the world has changed much, especially as regards the idea of decency.

On the eve of the 21st century, it is possible to sunbathe naked almost everywhere, like the ancient Greeks or Renaissance Susannahs, and this is not hailed as a return to the past, but as the hard-won result of claim and struggle.

Nowadays anything goes!

In this chaos of freedom and permissiveness, it is amazing to learn that in Trieste there is still a bathing-establishment in which the sexes are anachronistically separated by a wall, and men and women find it completely relaxing to sunbathe with members of their own sex, thus avoiding implications or complications of psychological and sexual nature.

It is evident that liyng naked in the sun is no longer a moral problem, but it can be a risk for one's health: pollution from industrial and biological discharges and the release into the sea of oil, mercury, nitrities, caesium and salmonella germs bring about necrobiotic and eurotrophic consequences.

People walk on the sand with shoes or boots in order not to dirty or infect themselves, they watch a sea where

170.

bathing is forbidden, stand on radioactive beaches where one must not play (remember Chernobyl?), hide themselves from the sun, whose dangerous rays are no longer filtered by an atmosphere torn and riddled by nebulized gases - is this to be mankind's future?

It is perhaps in anticipation of all this that the bathing-costume changes more and more, and turns from sports accessory into a real garment: the "costume" as a dressing-up, created without any restraint to fantasy or eclecticism, learned quotations or ethnic nostalgia.

In 1987 the old *Annette Kellerman* overall is revived: people don't wear itto dive into the mucilaginous sea, but for water sports and water-sky exhibitions, while the precious bodysuits in laminated materials covered with strass are all the rage for nights by the pool, for bathing after the disco, and for parties at beach-houses… in California.

168. It looks like a magic ritual, but it perfectly expresses the "ethnical" taste of the one-piece bathing-suit design. Sabbia, 1986.

169. Lycra bikini with band-brasserie and raphia applications on the hips. La Perla.

170. This one-piece bathing-suit captures and reflects the glow of sun and sea. Parah, 1987.

171.

172.

A CALL TO ORDER: THE NINETIES

Beach-collections for 1990 are still significantly influenced by the mistrust-atmosphere caused by two decades of reckless pollution: the leading-role is played by a "multifunctional" bathing-suit with coordinated accessories.

Parah's vice-president Gregory Piazzalunga, as well as the other leading beachwear manufacturers, have no doubts: bathing-suits are not just for diving into the sea, but can be worn on the beach as well as on ships and at summer night parties. And, following this philosophy, swimsuits are always transformable into gaudy mini-dresses for romantic rendezvous on the brink of the water - be it a pool, a river, a lake or the sea- and presented with special and daring accessories: long gloves and sensual black stockings, silk-fringed blouses, synthetic and shiny optical, ethnical or sideral costume jewellery, see-through gauze or golden network beachrobes, and large brimmed hats.

And if, owing to pollution, bathing-costumes run the risk of being worn less and less in the open air, they can be transformed and reinvented to suit new situations: people wear them at fitness centers, where they pass from one beauty-cabin to the other, from one equipment to the other, from the body-building room to the aerobics-class, and watch themselves in a mirror that reflects a well sculptured and firm body, according to the new standards of beauty. The sun-tan at all costs is out: new make-up rules suggest a natural complexion and amber body; at the fitness center people "sunbathe" under UVA lamps, considered less harmful than the sick sun.

The bathing-costume is still so important that it is the subject of the Monographic Course of the History of Clothes held by the author at the Faculty of Letters and Philosophy in Udine. The texts of the course ended with these words:" What is the future of the 'bathing-costume', a definition that is semantically and phonetically quite out of date? It will be worn less and less on beaches, rivers and in the water, where it will soon be wiser to wear skin-tight diver's suits, anatomical and biothecnical capsules, and science-fiction clothing to defend, protect and safeguard our bodies. Perhaps it will end its not very long history by becoming a collector's item".

Meanwhile, the London runways for the 1991 season launch Helen Storey's rigid-plastic-cup brasserie with vynil shorts and transparent plastic blouse to match, Vivienne Westwood's découpage one-piece costumes, and Red or Dead's red two-piece inspired to the '40s, except for the amount of leg shown.

On the other hand, the message from the Paris Fashion Shows for the same year leaves no space to extravagant show-offs: it seems to tune in with the emerging trend, a sort of "call to order", in a decade perceived like the eve of the new millennium, that brings along the urge to exorcize anxieties for the unknown, as well as the hope for a better future.

Hermes revises the two-piece, with Saint Tropez bodice and shorts to cover the hips, and Karl Lagerfel, the heir of Coco Chanel, places in his one-pieces the rigour and clear-cut lines typical of the famous Mademoiselle of High Fashion.

173.

171. The extremely sportive two-piece by Hermes plays about with the styles of the past. Hermes.
Collezioni prêt-a-porter, n. 20, 1991.

172. The unmistakable beacwear signed by two intertwined "C". Chanel.
Collezioni accessori, n. 10, 1992-93.

173. A dressy one-pice costume with a sash-belt that evidences the waist and enhances the hips.
Sabbia, 1992.

174. Strapless Lycra two-piece with applications.
Impronte di Parah, 1993.

174.

175.   176.   177.

WHAT COSTUME FOR WHAT TO-MORROW?

The economic crisis that shook the Western World at the beginning of the '90s put most of the present values under discussion and seemed to cause much political after-tought, social uproar, ecological repentance. Together with the will to make up for the mistakes made, and to regain credibility and honesty, the new moral attitude encourages reforms and improvement projects, as well as a stronger social fellowship at all levels.

Professionists who did not make up their skills on the spur of the moment and earned their job day after day, are able to resist and overcome the difficulties of such a hard moment, while in the whirlwind of events, the outlook for the future turns out to be less bleak than it had been depicted. Suddenly the last words of the monographical course sound anachronistic and obsolete, even if pronounced not long ago.

The ideal of female beauty evolves towards a more striking model: big breasts, voluminous buttocks, sensual and fleshy lips. Spas and fitness centers are all the rage, and so is plastic surgery; silicone manufacturers make more and more money in a whirlwind of diatribes, lawsuits, consents and retractions.

Those who can not afford new breasts make up with a miracle-working bikini, like the one launched by Cole at the Hawaii in 1992, with the upper part containing two bladders covered with soft plastic, inflatable by means of a mini-pump put in the middle of the bra. "You can pull it up or leave it down", states the ad, informing that every woman can adjust her measures as she wishes.

Although bathing-costumes still fall into three main cathegories - the traditional olympic style, the one-piece easily transformable into a mini-dress with corset-style strings, and the two-piece with strapless bra, triangle- or demi-bra or wired Saint Tropez corset - starting from Summer 1994, collections are generally renewed, both in the lines and in the technical solutions created for the maximum flexibility of use and made

178.   179.   180.

possible by a deep technical skill.

To the advantage of bathing-costume manufacturers and wearers, Eurojersey Inc create their latest innovation: a new patented synthetic fibre combination of "Multi microfibra Confort", the most sophisticated type of polyamide produced by Nylstar, and the Lycra elastomer by Du Pont. It is called Sensitive, and feels like a second skin, new in composition and structure, it has the aspect of a woven fabric and the functionality of jersey. It is close-fitting to the body without constricting it, allowes a better perspiration and dries quickly. Parah defines it "the new generation of bathing-suit material" and employs it for a whole collection.

New and creative versions of the old bathing-costume are launched: small-scale grandma-style bathing-suits, with embroidered flounces, draperies and formal hound's-tooth checks; reinforced costumes with silk tulle Lycra linings - for sirens trapped in the gilded nets of wealthy yachtsmen - and Lycra lined one- or two-piece bathing-suits that substain the figure in the crucial points and meet

the latest requirements of beach elegance.

But if the future of the bathing-suit is guaranteed by new ideas and materials, the new millenium will bring forth wetsuits made of slippery thermoregulating scales changing shades; and epidermic-microfibre bodysuits filtrating ultra-violet rays to bask in the now friendly and safe sun.

175.-177. From the Paris runways three models by Karl Lagerfeld for three different labels. Karl Laagerfeld for Chloé, K. Lagerfeld and Chanel.
Collezioni Donna, n. 43, 1995.

178. Soft microfibre for the essential bikini with linen shirt to match. La Perla, 1994.

179. Statuesque line for the two-piece, with the same trimming motif on bra and slip. Parah, 1994.

180. Siren-style one-piece bathing-costume with solar colours. The bra is lined, or "cought" in net. Parah, 1995

181. Ambitious and career-oriented, resolute and aggressive: the woman of the '90s is always in a hurry and busy, but on the beach she abandons herself to an ever-present desire for femininity wearing a sensual immaculate-white two-piece full of nostalgic laces. Parah 1995.

APPENDIX

GLOSSARY

ENGLISH

Bath-robe *A garment in cloth or towelling usually worn to dry oneself after bathing*

Bathing-cap *Generally in rubber, close-fitting; to protect the hair while bathing*

Bathing-suit *Garment designed to swim or bathe*

Beach-robe *Ample and practical garment of various styles, worn over bathing-costumes in matching fabric and/or colour*

Bikini *Scanty bathing-suit made up of bra and slip launched in 1946*

Bra *The upper part of the bikini or two-piece costume*

Burnous *Hooded cloak of Arabic tradition*

Cape *Sleeveless cloak to lay over the shoulders. Generally made of towelling for the beach.*

Dressing-gown *Long and completely open garment worn over bathing-suits at the beach during the '20s and '30s*

Eye-veil *Light veil made of gauze or small-net tulle used by ladies at the beginning of the century to protect themselves from the sun*

Flounced tail *The piece of cloth that in the one-piece bathing-suit covered the hips*

Lastex *Registered name for a special elasti fabric derived from rubber and manufactured with different synthetic fibres*

Lycra *Synthetic fibre introduced by Du Pont in 1958, from which many elastic and strong beachwear-fabrics are derived*

Microfibres *Multilobate-section fibres, whose base-elements have a diameter 10 times as small as that of traditional fibres. High-definition textile products are derived.*

Monokini *The bikini slip. Initially it was made up by clinging shorts held up by braces crossed over the bare chest.*

Olympic-style bathing-suit *Close-fitting jersey one-piece bathing-costume with wide braces, designed for olympic swimmers*

One-piece bathing-suit *A costume made of one single piece in different styles*

Overall *A combination of shirt and trousers sewn together, launched by futurist designer Thayaht*

Pareo *Piece of cloth, usually in cotton, knotted round the hips. Much used in Africa and Polinesia*

Polyamide *Nylon-derived synthetic fibres, very much used for bathing-suits*

Pyjama *Get-up made up by jacket and long flowing wide-bottomed trousers. Very fashionable on the beaches of the '30s*

Reinforced bathing-suit *One-piece bathing-suit with special inner linings and stratagems that make the figure look slimmer*

Rompers *One-piece bathing-costume made of cloth, with puffed trousers*

Saint Tropez *Short-sleeved bodice fastened under the breasts that leaves stomach and waist bare. To be worn with skirt and/or trousers*

Sash *A sort of scarf-belt knotted at the waist*

Schiavonetto *Wide and light clothing used by Venetian women to sunbathe on roof-terraces and to bleach their hair*

Serge *Diagonal-woven fabric in cotton or wool*

Stockings *In the finest cotton or light wool, they were worn with bathing -costumes at the beginning of the century*

Sunsuit *Cotton costume to wear at the beach; or suit with a very low neckline on the back*

Tanga *Two-piece costume with the slip leaving the bottom completely bare*

Towelling *Cotton or chenille fabric very soft and hairy, generally used for bath-robes and towels*

Turban *Fabric headgear draped in various styles*

Two-piece bathing-suit *A costume made of separate bra and slip*

ITALIANO	FRANCAIS	DEUTSCH	ESPANOL
Accappatoio	Peignoir - sortie de bain	Bademantel	Salida de baño
Cuffia da bagno	Bonnet de bain	Bademütze	Gorro de baño
Costume da bagno	Maillot de bain	Badeanzug	Bañador
Copricostume	Robe de plage	Strandkleid	Complemento de baño
Bikini	Bikini	Bikini	Bikini
Reggipetto	Soutien-gorge	Büstenhalter	Sostén
Burnous	Burnous	Bournous	Bournous
Cappa	Pélerine	Mantel	Capa
Vestaglia	Robe de plage	Strandanzug	Bata
Veletta	Voilette	Schleier	Velo
Faldino	Petit pan	Schösschen	Faldita
Lastex	Lastex	Lastex	Lastex
Lycra	Lycra	Lycra	Lycra
Microfibre	Microfibres	Microfibres	Microfibre
Monokini	Monokini	Monokini	Monokini
Olimpionico	Maillot de style olympien	Schwimmanzug	Maillot
Costume intero	Maillot une pièce	Einteil Badeanzug	Taje de baño
Tuta	Combinaison	Overall	Mono
Pareo	Pareo	Pareo	Pareo
Poliamide	Polyamide	Polyamide	Polyamide
Pyjamas	Pyjamas	Marlene Dietrich Hose	Pijama
Modellatore	Bustier	Badeanzun mit Korsage drin	Bañador armado
Pagliaccetto	Barboteuse	Hemdhose	Payaso
Saint Tropez	Saint Tropez	Strandleibchen	Saint Tropez
Fusciacca	Echarpe	Schärpe	Faja
Schiavonetto	Robe d'été d'antan	Antikes Sonnenkleid	Schiavonetto
Sergia	Serge	Köper	Sarga
Calze	Bas	Strümfe	Medias
Prendisole	Bain de soleil	Sonnenkleid	Tomasol
Tanga	Tanga - slip brésilen	Tanga	Tanga
Spugna	Tissu éponge	Frottee	Esponja
Turbante	Turbant	Turban	Turbante
Costume due pezzi	Maillot deux pièces	Zweiteilen Badeanzug	Dos piezas

BIBLIOGRAPHY

BOOKS

1831 - G. Ferrario *Il costume antico e moderno di tutti i popoli*, Vincenzo Batelli, Firenze

1891 - P. Schivardi, *I bagni di mare*, Treves, Milano

1904 - G. Pauly, *Gainsborough*, Klosing, Leipzig

1905 - G. Mourey, *Gainsborough*, Laurens, Paris

1912 - P. Mantegazza, *Igiene della bellezza*, Milano

1948 - E. Bondensen, *Den nye strikkebeken*, Oslo

1948 - F. Cappi Bentivegna, *Storia del costume da bagno* da L'*Illustrazione italiana* num. spec., Milano

1948 - J. Laver, *Taste and Fashion*, Thames and Hudson, London

1957 - Laver Dress, *The changing shape of things*, Thames and Hudson, London

1958 - E. Waterhause, Gainsborough, Hilton, London

1963 - A. Bony, *Les Années '60*, Editions di Régard, Paris

1963 - M. Braun, Ronsdorf, *The weel of fashion*, Thames and Hudson, London

1963 - N. Bradfield, *Historical Costume of England*, London

1963 - Gernsheim, *Fashion and reality 1840 - 1814*, Faber & Faber, London

1968 - G.C. Argan, *Storia dell'arte italiana*, Sansoni, Firenze

1969 - J. Laver, *Modesty in dress*, Thames and Hudson, London

1969 - R. Levy Pisetzky, *Storia del costume in Italia*, vol. 5°, Treccani I.E.I., Milano

1970 - L. Kybalovà, O. Erbenovà, M. Lamanovà, *Encyclopedie illustrée du costume et de la mode*, Gründ, Paris

1976 - M. Battersby, *La mode Art Déco*, Flammarion, Paris

1976 - Y. Deslandres, *Le costume image de l'homme*, Albin Michel, Paris

1977 - G. Novello, *Il signore di buona famiglia*, Mondadori, Milano

1979 - A. Beltrami, *Identikit del '900 attra verso la moda*, Centro SMC, Milano

1979 - R. Lebeck, *Bitte, recht freundlich*, Harenberg Kommunikation, Dortmund

1980 - G. Butazzi, *1922-1943 vent'anni di moda italiana*, Centro D, Firenze

1980 - P. Devlin, *Vogue 1920-1980*, Idealibri, Milano

1981 - R. Del Lungo, *Spogliare la nonna*, Colosci, Cortona

1981 - P. Perrot, *Il sopra e il sotto della borghesia*, Longanesi, Milano

1981 - C. Probert, *Swimwear in Vogue since 1910*, Abbeville Press, New York

1981 - G.M. Trevelyan, *Storia della società inglese*, Einaudi, Torino

1981 - I. Zanier, *Venezia Archivio Naja*, Venezia

1982 - N. Aspesi, *Il lusso e l'autarchia*, Rizzoli, Milano

1982 - E. Charles Roux, *Chanel and her world*, Weidenfeld and Nicholson, London

1982 - P. Glynn, *Pelle a pelle*, Gremese, Roma

1982 - D. Kunzle, *Fashion and fetishism*, Totowa, New Jersey

1983 - R. Gaudriault, *La gravure de mode féminine en France*, Les éditions de l'amateur, Paris

1983 - G. Mosca *Viva il Re*, Rizzoli, Milano

1983 - W. Parker *I grandi disegnatori di Vogue*, Milano

1984 - S. Blum, *Designs by Erté... from Harper's Bazaar*, Dover Publications, New York

1984 - M. Colmer, *Bathing beauties*, London

1984 - J. Peacock, *Fashion sketchbook*, London

1984 - G. Comisso, *Agenti segreti a Venezia*, Longanesi, Milano

1985 - J. Grislam, M. Le Blanc, *Aux fils du temps de la redoute*, Paris

1985 - F. Kennet, *Secrets of the couturiers*, Orbis, London

1986 - E. Crispolti, *Il futurismo e la moda*, Marsilio, Venezia

1986 - Y. Deslandres, *Paul Poiret 1789-1944*, Editions du régard, Paris

1986 - F. Falluel, *Sportbekleidung* da *Anziehungskräfte: 1786-1986*, Stadtmuseum, München

1986 - P. White, *Elsa Schiaparelli*, Aurum Press, London

1986 - P. Steinbach Palazzini, *Coca Cola superstar*, Idealibri, Milano

1987 - G. Garnier, *Paris Couture Années Trente*, Paris

1988 - C.M. Calasibetta *Fairchild's Dictionary of Fashion* II ediz., Fairchild Pubblications New York

1988 - G. Triani, *Pelle di luna, pelle di sole*, Marsilio, Venezia

1990 - R. Panuzzo J. Valli a cura *Il diziona rio della moda* di Georgina O'Hara, Zanichelli, Bologna
1991 - S. Kennedy, *Pucci a Renaissance in Fashion* - Abbeville Press, New York

CATALOGUES

1919 - *Catalogo di vendita Coen*, Roma
1923 - *Abiti estivi* (cat. di vendita per corri spondenza), Milano
1980 - W. Rubin, *Pablo Picasso*, New York
1981 - G. Butazzi a cura, *Mostra del costume dell'epoca Dannunziana*, Fondazione Il Vittoriale, Brescia
1985 - *Abiti e costumi futuristi*, Comune di Pistoia
1986 - *Moda a Trieste*, Trieste
1987 - *Lido di oggi*, Lido di allora, Venezia
1988 - P. Dini, *La donna e la moda nella pit tura del secondo '800*, Comune di Montecatini Terme
1989 - *Lido e lidi*, Marsilio, Venezia

MAGAZINES

1856 - 1875: *La Ricamatrice*, Milano
1865 - 1889: *Journal des demoiselles*, Paris
1865: *La mode illustrée*, Paris
1872 - 1876: *La Novità*, Milano
1877: *Il bazar*, Milano
1879 - 1882: *Bazaar*, Berlin
1879 - 1899: *Margherita*, Milano
1884: *Illustrierte Frauen Zeitung*, Berlin
1891: *Moniteur des dames*, Paris
1895 - 1914: *La stagione*, Milano
1895: *New York world*, New York
1896 - 1899: *La revue de la mode*, Paris
1897: *La nouvelle mode*, nn. 26. 37, Paris
1898 - *Natura ed arte*, Milano
1898 - 1922: *La mode illustrée*, Paris
1900: *La saison*, Paris
1902 - 1933: *La lettura*, Milano
1903: *The Strand magazine*, London
1905 - 1912: *Regina*, Napoli
1906: *La mode pratique*, Paris
1909 - 1928: *La moda illustrata*, Milano
1909 - 1938: *Fémina*, Paris
1910 - 1922: *La gazette du bon ton*, Milano
1912: *Journal des demoiselles*, n. 7, Paris
1915: *La vie parisienne*, Paris
1917 - 1919: *Pictorial review*, New York
1918 - 1939: *Vogue*, Paris

1919 - 1925: *Rivista balneare*, Venezia
1925 - 1934: *Lidel*, Milano
1927: *Scena illustrata*, nn. 18, 19, Firenze
1928: *Femenil*, 19 nov., Madrid
1928 - 1940: *Le jardin des modes*, Paris
1929: *El hogar, junio*, Buenos Ayres
1931: *Figaro artistique illustré*, Paris
1933: *Mani di fata*, giugno, Milano
1934: *Modes et travaux*, n. 346, Paris
1934 - 1935: *La donna, la casa, il bambino*, Milano
1936 - 1942: *Dea*, Milano
1938 - 1960: *Venezia permanenze al Casinò*, Venezia
1939 - 1964: *Grazia*, Milano
1939 - 1966: *La donna*, Milano
1940: *Rakam*, Milano
1943: *Fili moda*, n. 32, Milano
1946 - 1947: *Album de la mode du Figaro*, nn. 9,10, Paris
1948: *L'illustrazione italiana*, spec. moda, Milano
1948 - 1949: *Plaisir de France*, Paris
1949: *Elle*, n.197, Paris
1949: *Venezia - Lido*, Venezia
1950: *Donne d'oggi*, n.2, Milano
1950: *La settimana Incom*, Roma
1950 - 1965: *Mani di fata*, Milano
1951: *Donne eleganti*, Milano
1951 - 1953: *La familia*, Mexico City
1952: *Die elegante Linie*, n. 2, Berlin
1952 - 1960: *Novità*, Milano
1953: *Bellezza*, n. 5, Milano
1956: *Il giorno*, 25 aprile, Milano
1957: *Annabella*, n. 32 11 agosto, Milano
1958: *Tempo*, 27 marzo, Milano
1959: *Vogue*, may, New York
1961: *Lo specchio*, Roma
1962: *Amica*, nn. 17, 13, Milano
1965: *Annabelle*, 7 Juli, Zürich
1967: *Life magazine*, New York
1967 - 1989: *Vogue Italia*, Milano
1969: *Harper's Bazaar*, Mai, Berlin
1970 - 1971: *Linea intima*, s.l.
1976: *Il femminile*, Venezia
1977: *Marie Claire*, n.297, Mai, Paris
1986: *Gente Mese*, n.8, Milano
1987: *Moda*, suppl. Corsera, n. 21, Milano
1987: *La Repubblica*, (8.11.15.17.19 ag.) Roma
1987: *La Repubblica*, suppl. n. 53, Roma
1988 - 1994: *Fashion*, Milano
1988: *Corriere della sera*, 11 agosto, Milano
1991: *Collezioni prêt-à-porter*, n. 20, Modena
1992: *Accessori collezioni*, n. 10, Modena
1995: *Collezioni donna*, n. 43, Modena

INDEX OF NAME

Legend: NN = page *NN* = caption

134

Fotolito: Articolor - Verona
Paper: Burgo Distribuzione - Assago Milano
Printed in march,1995 by Grafica Editoriale S.p.A. - Bologno

BERKELEY COLLEGE LIBRARY/WESCHESTER

3 6615 4000 9702 1

**CARDS MUST REMAIN IN THIS
POCKET AT ALL TIMES**
a charge will be made for
lost or damaged cards

**BERKELEY COLLEGE
WESTCHESTER CAMPUS LIBRARY**
99 Church Street
White Plains, NY 10601